WOMEN MYSTICS

LOUIS BOUYER

Women Mystics

HADEWIJCH OF ANTWERP
TERESA OF AVILA
THÉRÈSE OF LISIEUX
ELIZABETH OF THE TRINITY
EDITH STEIN

Translated by
Anne Englund Nash

Foreword by
Kris McGregor

IGNATIUS PRESS   SAN FRANCISCO

Title of the French original:
Figures mystiques féminines
© 1989 by Les Editions du Cerf, Paris

Cover images (including colorized black & white photographs)
In order of appearance, from left to right:

Edith Stein (*Teresa Benedicta of the Cross*)
Passport photo (ca. 1939)
Cologne Carmel Archives
Wikimedia Commons Image

Elizabeth of the Trinity
photograph
Wikimedia Commons Image

Teresa of Avila
Painting by Peter Paul Reubens (1577–1640)
Kunsthistoriches Museum, Wien
Wikimedia Commons Image

Hadewijch of Antwerp
Painting (as she has been imagined)
Provenance unknown

Thérèse of Lisieux
Carmel of Lisieux
photograph
© Office Central de Lisieux

Cover design by Enrique J. Aguilar

© 1993, 2022 by Ignatius Press, San Francisco
All rights reserved
ISBN 978-1-62164-555-9 (PB)
ISBN 978-1-64229-202-2 (eBook)
Library of Congress Control Number 2021953188
Printed in the United States of America ∞

To the very dear memory
of Hedwige d'Ursel
Marquise de Maupeou Monbail

CONTENTS

Foreword by Kris McGregor 9
Introduction 13

I. Hadewijch of Antwerp 17

The Discovery of Hadewijch 21
Exemplarism: Its Properly "Hadewigian"
    Meaning 28
The Generosity and Purity of Love 35
Perspective on God and Christ 38
Flow of Love of Neighbor and Ebb of Love into
    God 46
The Birth of Christ in Us 49

II. From Hadewijch to Eckhart and Ruusbroec 55

From Hadewijch I to Hadewijch II 55
Position of Meister Eckhart 58
Speculative Developments and Spiritual
    Enlightenments 70
Ruusbroec: Heir and Illuminator of
    the Hadewigian Tradition 74
From Tauler to Angelus Silesius 85

III. Teresa of Avila 91

From the Mystics of the North to the Mystics
    of Spain 91
The Career of Teresa of Avila 96
The Teaching of the *Vida* 102

The Discalced Carmelite Friars: Between
John of the Cross and Gracian. 109
Last Teachings of Teresa III

IV. From Teresa to John of the Cross 115

The Life of John of the Cross 115
The Thought of John of the Cross 119
Origin of the Doctrine of Saint John of
the Cross 123

V. Thérèse of Lisieux 133

Three Carmelites for Our Times 133
Thérèse of the Child Jesus and of the
Holy Face. 134
From *Histoire d'une âme* to the *Écrits
autobiographiques*. 140
Love, Little Way and Darkness of Faith 142
The Gospel of the Father and the Mystery of
the Cross 146

VI. Elizabeth of the Trinity 155

The Carmelite Vocation and Life of
Elizabeth Catez. 155
Elizabeth and Thérèse 158
"Laudem Gloriae" 160
Our Life in the Trinity 168

VII. Edith Stein 173

Edith Stein's Position 173
The Achievement of Edith Stein 182
"Ultima Verba" 186

Conclusion 189

FOREWORD

Pope Benedict XVI gave a series of Wednesday audiences about remarkable, holy women of the Middle Ages. Some of them had been overlooked for too long because their mysticism could not be easily categorized—women such as Hildegard of Bingen, whom the pope later canonized and proclaimed a Doctor of the Church, Matilda of Hackeborn, Gertrude the Great, Marguerite d'Oingt and Angela Foligno. Most of the women were largely unknown, and their liberation from the vaults of obscurity has rounded out our understanding of the "feminine genius" described by Pope John Paul II and its contribution to the Church. "Theology can receive a special contribution from women because they can talk about God and the mysteries of faith using their particular intelligence and sensitivity", said Benedict XVI. "I, therefore, encourage all those who carry out this service to do it with a profound ecclesial spirit, nourishing their reflection with prayer and looking to the great riches, not yet fully explored, of the medieval mystic tradition."

A pioneer in that theological sensitivity was Father Louis Bouyer. A French Lutheran minister who entered the Catholic Church in 1939, he became a priest of the Oratory of Jesus and Mary Immaculate, which is based on but distinct from the Oratory of Saint Philip Neri. Author of numerous books on the sacramental and spiritual life, many of which are considered classics, Father Bouyer had a profound knowledge and understanding of mysticism.

It was shortly after Pope Benedict's Wednesday audiences described above that I found a copy of Father Bouyer's *Women Mystics*, originally published in 1993 by Ignatius Press, in a friend's library in Rome. I knew both men to be colleagues in founding, along with others, the highly regarded theological journal *Communio*, so I was eager to read Father Bouyer's commentary on the famous Carmelites Teresa of Avila, Thérèse of Lisieux and Elizabeth of the Trinity (canonized by Pope Francis in 2016), as well as Edith Stein (Teresa Benedicta of the Cross, canonized by Pope John Paul II in 1998). I was surprised to find Stein among the women because I had never seen her described as a mystic, and I had never even heard of Hadewijch, a thirteenth-century Belgian laywoman. How did she connect with these Carmelites, I wondered. I was very intrigued.

As I zealously tore into the book, I soon found myself stuck in the dense theological groundwork laid out in the first two chapters, which Father Bouyer warns is rich in "historico-critical or metaphysical considerations". A reader might be tempted to take up his suggestion in the last paragraph of his introduction to begin with chapter 3, "Teresa of Avila". But I would encourage the reader to begin at the beginning! There lies a golden thread in the first two chapters that Father Bouyer uses to connect all things and persons in the end. The reader should take whatever time is needed to be taught by a spiritual master.

Although this book is dedicated to women mystics, three important men are discussed at length: Meister Eckhart, a German Dominican scholar; Blessed John of Ruusbroec, a Flemish Augustinian; and Saint John of the Cross. The first two are part of the story of Hadewijch of Antwerp, who was underappreciated for centuries because her writings were often combined with writings from an unknown woman who is now identified as Hadewijch II. Why did it take nearly six hundred years for the actual works of Hadewijch to be properly identified? Father Bouyer tackles this question and sets the record straight. He discusses John of the Cross because of his partnership with Teresa of Avila in their sixteenth-century reform of the Carmelite Order. As the reader will discover, Father Bouyer is all about connections. In discussing important relationships, he demonstrates the complementarity of male and female in the life of the Church. One cannot function properly without the other, and one is not superior to the other.

Father Bouyer's text is filled with dynamic energy. He may densely pack a page, but each is filled with enthusiasm for the subject. This book has more exclamation points than any other I have read on spirituality. (In his fondness for this punctuation mark, I think Father Bouyer can be matched only by Teresa of Avila herself!)

Yet the great professor does not suffer sentimentality well. With his rapier wit, he often expresses his thoughts sharply. Some readers, especially devotees of Thérèse of Lisieux and Elizabeth of the Trinity, might find some of his comments too harsh. I was a bit chagrined by some of his statements about the Martin family, the Carmel of Lisieux and the poetic expression of the two young Carmelites. But I found that he does indeed respect these saints. He tears down certain images and conceptions of them in order to build them back up on a stronger foundation, one that allows them to mirror more truly the very heart of Divine Love.

Father Bouyer's deep admiration for Teresa of Avila and Teresa Benedicta of the Cross is inspiring, and so is his reverence for the tender expression of faith and hope articulated by Hadewijch of Antwerp and Elizabeth of the Trinity. But most moving for this reader is his bending of the knee to the Little Flower of Carmel, who, as he says, "is indeed the Saint that we need".

Kris McGregor
Feast of Saint Ignatius of Loyola
July 31, 2021

INTRODUCTION

Our age seems characterized by, among many other ambiguous human phenomena, an almost sudden awareness of the importance of the role of women in all civilization and of a singular deficiency shown by our own time in this regard. It is all the more unfortunate that, until now, the so-called women's liberation movement resulting from this does not seem able to imagine any other liberation of women than that which consists in making her into a pseudo-male!

The whole women's liberation movement would now do well to avoid making increasingly worse—indeed, making irremediable—an assuredly unjust situation with respect to women, a situation that, for men themselves, represents only an apparent victory, for neither of the two sexes can be fully itself without the other.

One of the errors that has tainted this movement up to now and has led it into such misunderstandings is the false idea—which is unfortunately too often an *idée fixe*!—that the inferior condition of the woman in modern civilization is a legacy of Christianity, and very particularly of the Bible, as much of the New Testament as of the Old. A strange historical error pointed out by a woman and a first-rate scholar, Régine Pernoud.[1] For, as she has found, quite the contrary is true. Judaism laid the groundwork for the recognition of equality in the difference between woman and man, and it

[1] See, in particular, her book *Women in the Days of Cathedrals*, trans. Anne Côté-Harris (San Francisco: Ignatius Press, 1998).

was Christianity that succeeded in giving it positive defini-
tion. The sense of women's inferiority in the modern age
appears to be one of the most harmful results of dechris-
tianization. This situation is due particularly to the return,
which was begun here in France with the legists of Philip
the Fair, to Roman pagan law, which was substituted for
medieval legislation penetrated by the biblical and evangelical spirit. The Napoleonic Code, making the woman a perpetual minor, was to push things to the extreme. And, it
must be repeated, if the present so-called women's liberation movement were to continue for some time along its
current path, it is impossible to see it doing anything but
consummating this regression.

In fact, in the Church, from the very outset women
have played a role that, though different from that of men,
appeared only the more indispensable and even precisely
fundamental. To go back to its very beginnings, it was undoubtedly the apostles to whom Christ gave the mission of
proclaiming with authority, in his own name, the gospel
of the Resurrection. But it was from women that they received the content of that gospel. In fact, there is no doubt
that women were the first to believe it, and it was in being
obliged to recognize the truth in spite of themselves that
the apostles came to propagate the faith. Better still: Christ
himself, to be sure, is the sole Savior of mankind, but it is
just as certain—and the Fathers of the Church as well as
all medieval theologians are in agreement about it—that if
there had not first been a woman, Mary, who freely con-
sented to become the mother of the Savior, then Christ, as
God made man in order to save mankind, could not even
have come into existence.

In the Church, in all ages, women have therefore had a
role—a role quite different, to be sure, from that entrusted

to men, but one without which the men's role could not have been carried out. The sole goal of the present book is to show, through deeds and texts, that the same is true very particularly for the Church of modern times with respect to the heart of her Christian vitality: that is, the effective practice of an authentic Christian spirituality. If the decadence of medieval Scholasticism and then the interwoven mistaken ideas of the Renaissance and the Protestant Reformation were unable to strike a mortal blow against that Church, this was above all to the credit of a succession of exceptional feminine personalities. We shall try to establish this by studying some of those whose influence and sustained tradition, continually renewed, seem to have been decisive in that regard. This study will concentrate on Hadewijch of Antwerp, Teresa of Avila, Thérèse of the Child Jesus, Elizabeth of the Trinity and Edith Stein. We could have added others, like Saint Catherine of Genoa, on the edge of modern times, or Adrienne von Speyr, so close to our own. But we have confined ourselves to these five figures because the continuity from one of them to another, though an ever-creative continuity, is striking.

To sum up in a few words the specifically feminine and absolutely fundamental contribution of these five women, it is particularly their tradition that has led modern Christians (those, at least, who have understood the lesson of these women) from idle speculations or sentimental devotions to the reality of the Christian experience in its purity, which is inseparable from its fecundity. The whole objective, the whole meaning of what follows is not really to prove this, so to speak, but simply to show it by letting them speak as much as possible for themselves and by freeing their progressive testimony from all that might conceal its victorious continuity.

Readers who are not perhaps directly interested in either historico-critical or metaphysical considerations might begin their reading at Chapter Three. If they would later like to assure themselves of the fidelity of our modern mystics to both ancient tradition and orthodoxy, they could then return to the first two chapters.

I

HADEWIJCH OF ANTWERP

The twelfth and thirteenth centuries were marked by a prodigious rebirth throughout the entire Christian West of the great tradition, inseparably intellectual and spiritual, of those we call the Fathers of the Church. During this period there was a rediscovery of those theologians who had been moved by the inspiration of the Church of the martyrs, continuing into that of the first monks, theologians who profited from the peace that was for the first time assured to the Church in order, from that inspiration, to enter into everything in the Greek philosophical tradition that might retain permanent value. The thirteenth century, however, saw the advent of what could be called Scholasticism,[1] that is, Christian thought whose source was no longer the monasteries themselves, or monasteries revitalized by their own sources, but the first universities. These were schools that could be described as secular, not only because of their establishment in the great urban centers but also because of their determination to produce an intellectual formation aimed at the building of a human city, even if still impregnated by Christianity, and no longer solely the City of God.

---

[1] On the renaissance of the twelfth century, see Dom Déchanet, *Aux sources de la spiritualité de Guillaume de Saint-Thierry* (Bruges, 1940), and Dom Jean LeClercq, *L'Amour des lettres et le désir de Dieu* (Paris, 1957). On the thirteenth century, M.-D. Chenu, *La Theologie comme science au XIIIe siècle* (Paris, 1957). There would also be great profit in reading Newman, *Historical Sketches*, volume III: *Universities*, particularly chapter XV, pp. 192ff., which will be contrasted with *The Benedictine Schools*, pp. 431ff. in volume II.

From then on, the theologian himself was going to become a specialist, a neighbor and essentially a competitor with jurists, doctors and other professionals of the aforementioned city. Among the latter, the philosopher, one who knows no other rule of the true but the application of reason to common experience, following the example of Aristotle as transmitted by the Arabs, would not be long in coming forward as his competitor par excellence. Thus there would be the greatest temptation for the medieval and postmedieval theologian to get the better of the philosopher by modeling himself on the latter, as it were, in such a way as to make theology itself fall within the scope of an a priori, systematic philosophy.

The greatest Christian thinkers of the century, like Albert the Great, Thomas Aquinas and Duns Scotus, by accepting this imposed scope and the challenge it implied, endeavored to maintain nevertheless the primacy of biblical revelation, of the word of God. One might say, in an unavoidable simplification, that Albert and his successors, the new Christian Neoplatonists of the German thirteenth century, would occupy themselves with reinfusing Aristotelian rationalism with the whole contribution of Platonic idealism christianized along the lines of Saint Augustine. With greater boldness, Duns Scotus would try to go beyond and draw Platonism as well as Aristotelianism into a thoroughly Christian personalism, dominated, as Origen's attempt had already been, by an absolutization of freedom, uncreated freedom, in God, as well as created freedom in us.

Thomas, at an equal distance from the two, would undertake a particularly bold synthesis, in the sense that it combines in God platonizing intellectualism with an overall Christian freedom and, for the created world, strives to inject this same Christian meaning into a basically Aristotelian vision of things. But what distinguishes him even more and raises him above his contemporaries, including the Augustinianism brilliantly revitalized by Bonaventure, is, in practice as in theory, his insistence on the fact that a theology thus acclimated, adapted to the philosophical imperialism of the day, if it is not to dissolve and lose itself, can only be an instrument for a richer understanding of the *sacra pagina*, to which it must not only constantly return but in the end submit itself.

None of all that, however, could check the increasingly exclusive intellectualism spread by the enthusiastic rediscovery of Aristotelianism. From the fourteenth century on, the divine freedom, the Christian individualism of Duns Scotus, caught up in this tidal wave, would degenerate into the *potentia absoluta* of Occam, that is, a vision of God in which his sovereignty was confused with arbitrariness. In other words, this wholly positive infinity of love of the Christian God, with him, returns to the *apeiron* such as Greek intellectualism conceived it, relegating God to the mere indefinite, as if that would be the liberation from all constraint.[2]

Faced with this trend, in the fourteenth century, the German Dominican school, keeping Albert and Thomas together, would devote themselves to saving the immanence as well as the transcendence of the Christian God by recapturing the paradoxes of Plotinian Neoplatonism, while charging them with a new meaning that, in Eckhart and his disciples, was evidently born of the spiritual experience of contemplative souls, women for the most part, for whom they had pastoral responsibility.[3]

This, in particular, accounts for that dizzying intellectual

---

[2] On all this, see É. Gilson, *La Philosophie et la théologie* (Paris, 1960).

[3] Cf. especially Alain de Libera, *Introduction à la mystique rhénane: d'Albert le Grand à Maître Eckhart*, (Paris: OEIL, 1984).

construction of Eckhart, which can already be read, as would again be the case with Nicolas of Cusa in the following century, either in the literal sense of an intellectualism that evaporates, that voids all reality, or in the exact opposite sense of a reality that trifles with all intellectualism by confining itself to the human hair-splitting of an absolutized logic.

Yet what is behind these wild paradoxes of Eckhartian thought, short of his apparent pantheism and beyond his unavoidably suspect nothingness? Undeniably an experience that proves to be inexhaustible with regard to all attempts at rationalization. Some have denied that this experience was his own and wish to see in it only an unbridled intellectualism, thinking thereby to be able to escape it.[4] But this view is incompatible with the tone, the conviction, in a word, the faith that exudes from all his sermons and other spiritual writings. This is not to say that he himself produced this experience himself as if at the end of his intensified logic. It is much rather that he had encountered it, had recognized the purity, the unmistakable reality of it and, having made it his own, had then tried, if not to link it with a wholly rational thought, at least to justify it, to clear its path. . . .

This is indeed what a discovery of the last half-century seems to have established. The paradoxes that at once underlie and extend beyond, transcend his thought, even if he most likely adopted them through his own experience, do not signify that this experience was a product of his speculation but indeed that he had found it, beyond doubt, and had been able to take possession of it only by opening himself, for his own part, to something beyond all thought that is only thought.

---

[4] I am thinking particularly of C. F. Kelley, *Meister Eckhart on Divine Knowledge* (New Haven, 1977).

All these paradoxes are actually not his creation. He holds them because of the contemplative spiritual milieu in which he worked. And there can no longer be any doubt about their source, more precisely, their first author. It was a woman, an exceptional contemplative, from one century prior to the theology that we would consider Eckhartian. This was Hadewijch of Antwerp, whose thought was relayed to Eckhart (thus "activating" him as a mystical writer, so to speak) by a scarcely less inspired disciple, who, for want of her real identity, has been called Hadewijch II.[5]

The Discovery of Hadewijch

While the first Hadewijch abruptly emerged, around the beginning of this century, from an obscurity in which she had remained buried for at least five centuries preceding our own, she is still very far from having revealed to us a precisely definable identity. But her exceptional personality takes form before our eyes with an irresistible vigor.

It was around the end of the nineteenth century that a manuscript was spotted in the Royal Library of Brussels that contained, among others, a series of poems in Flemish of an astonishing beauty. It was this quality of her language as well as her poetry, inspired by trouvères but with a very feminine, personal refinement, that first struck the philologists. The first to translate them into French was Maurice Maeterlinck. But it was only around the time of the First World

---

[5] On Hadewijch and Hadewijch II, the best introduction in English is the volume *Hadewijch: The Complete Works*, translated and with an excellent introduction and notes by Mother Columba Hart, O.S.B. (New York: Paulist, 1981). The Carthusian Dom J. B. Porion (who died in 1987) has also given good introductions and notes to his French translation, *Hadewijch d'Anvers, Poèmes des béguines* (Paris, 1954) and *Hadewijch, Lettres spirituelles* (Geneva, 1972).

War that specialists in spirituality, like Father Van Mierlo, S.J., then the Dominican Axters, perceived that what they had there was not only a work of unrivaled linguistic and literary interest but the testimony of a very great mystic.

At first, Hadewijch, whose name had finally been identified in a margin of the manuscript discovered first (another complete manuscript and then an incomplete one would successively come to light), was seen as the long-sought intermediary between Eckhart and Ruusbroec. A more extensive study, however, would reveal, according to what she herself said in letters or accounts of visions accompanying these poems, that she was undoubtedly contemporary with well-dated personalities, which obliges recognition of the fact that she was not at all a disciple of Eckhart but the most outstanding of his predecessors. In fact, there can no longer be any question of placing her later than the first half of the thirteenth century.

The same progress in these studies, on the other hand, led scholars to the belief that, among the poems collected in the first manuscript, some are later: hence the supposition of a "Hadewijch II", as she would be called, who was herself already developing the most dizzying of Eckhart's speculations on the unity beyond the Trinity into which the most advanced contemplatives plunge. But contemporary critics are now agreed in thinking that this second series of poems, far from depending on Eckhart, is actually translating one of those lucidly described experiences that inspired him!

In the meantime, there has also been the realization that Ruusbroec was familiar with what was most personal in Hadewijch's teaching and quotes verbatim several passages from her successor. What is more, John Leeuwen, the pious chef of Groenendael, his disciple, expressly praises the whole body of Hadewijch's work.

There can no longer be any doubt that we have here, if not Eckhart's sole sources, assuredly the most invaluable testimony about a spirituality developed well before him and on which he was closely dependent. But, above all, it follows that we have, in the person of Hadewijch, a spiritual master almost without equal as well as an exquisite feminine figure, endowed with the greatest gifts of intelligence and of heart as well as of culture.

The perfection of her language as well as of her literary form, the quality and breadth of her reading (it is clear that she read both Latin and French fluently) and, even more, her predilection for certain ideas, to begin with, nobility, as well as pride, clarity and generosity, have led to the belief that she came from an aristocratic milieu. But, even in her time, the great families of the Antwerp bourgeoisie had sufficient association with this milieu and soon surpassed it in matters of education.

Whatever her origins, it is obvious that she constitutes a transcendent example of the way in which the whole dialectic of profane love, certainly already influenced at its sources, with the Arabs themselves, by a religion that had borrowed its symbolism from human love, is transcended and consummated by a new change with respect to mystical experience.

As for the milieu to which she was attached and which was to remember her teaching, there can be no hesitation in recognizing that of the Beghards and Beguines who were spread particularly across the north of France, the Low Countries and the Rhineland. Especially from her letters, it is gathered that she played a considerable role in it, but not without having to suffer, and perhaps terribly, as much and more from the instability of this milieu as from the suspicions it could provoke. On the basis of some of her most moving texts, some have gone so far as to believe that she found herself rejected by some of her own disciples and forced to find refuge in some pious hospital, if she did not know an even more tragic end, like others among her contemporaries, such as Marguerite Poret, burned by an Inquisitor who had himself passed from heresy to an orthodoxy that was all the more suspicious.

But how to give a fair description of this milieu? There was above all an increasingly felt dissatisfaction, not only with respect to the old monastic order, more or less absorbed in feudalism, but just as much with regard to the Cistercian reform, which in less than a century had been corrupted by its overly rapid success, to say nothing of the Franciscans, already unfaithful to their founder during his lifetime, or of the Dominicans or Premonstratensians, whose decadence seems to have followed in the footsteps of development.

This was the reason for forming groups of laymen, men or women, firmly decided to remain in their secular state, while wishing to live the gospel to the depths, in the manner of the first Syrian ascetics or the first monks in Egypt, but easily succumbing, on the material plane as well as on the doctrinal, to their lack of organization. She is eminently characteristic of them in her insistence upon the impossibility of separating the love of God from fraternal charity, extending to everyone and not only to one's fellow sisters and brothers.

But she is distinguished by both the highly traditional and the powerfully original character of her teaching, in which the constant balance is no less striking than the depth, all bearing the indelible mark of a dazzling intelligence united to the freshest sensitivity. The wholly personal charm that comes through a literary form that is as spontaneous as it can be scholarly makes her expression entirely her own. Undoubtedly a saint, a great woman who is at the same time a great mind, but first of all a being with a unique transparency, such is this Hadewijch, who might have remained unknown but who could never have been confused with any other, not even her disciple, who was nevertheless scarcely less gifted in all respects but much more intellectual, with the limits that implies.

Hadewijch, however, through her visions (which have perhaps not been sufficiently studied by those who have analyzed her spiritual doctrine), remains very close to that apocalyptic neoprophetism made famous in the preceding century by Saint Hildegarde of Bingen,[6] Saint Elizabeth of Schönau, brought closer to her through Blessed Mechtilde of Magdeburg,[7] that Beguine whose life was to conclude, like others, in a Cistercian cloister. It is difficult to distinguish in these visions what is experience properly speaking from what remains an imaginative projection by psychologies much more concrete than ours have become, for whom intellectual culture is confused with abstraction. With Hadewijch as with her predecessors and contemporaries, this visionary genre accompanies an acute sense of a radical need for renewal, which will be capable of falling into the illusions of the disciples of Joachim of Flora. But, as in the Johannine Apocalypse itself, it is the properly spiritual experience that is the source as well as the immediate end. It is not, therefore, surprising that it is mixed with very personal reminiscences, nor that it affirms what will be as if the heart of Hadewijch's activity, definitively expressed in her

[6] Father Matthew Fox, O.P., well known in the United States, has produced a study about her. While often fanciful, like everything he writes, it nevertheless contains some very good observations.

[7] Jeanne Ancelet-Hustache has undoubtedly devoted the best study to her: *Mechtilde de Magdebourg* (Paris, 1926).

poems, explained in her letters. And this is, obviously, the
love of God and its development, expressed in the imagery
and vocabulary of courtly literature: that is, the wholly generous love with which he loves us, has loved us in his Son
from all eternity, calling forth the response in us of a totally
surrendered love.

It is here that the characteristic tests of courtly love are
introduced as an expression of the detachment, disinterestedness, abnegation without which love, in us as well as in
her, would never be worthy of that wholly divine love that
preceded it, arouses it and will fulfill it in consummated
union.

The visions, however, are attached to a curious document[8] that helps us to situate Hadewijch historically but
that has embarrassed her modern commentators more than
it should. She in fact expresses in it her preferences among
the saints and also lists there some of her contemporaries,
who are known to us in varying degrees, presenting them
perhaps a bit too liberally with halos. What is more, she does
not hesitate, it seems, to place herself along with some of
her closest friends in the highest celestial spheres. We too
easily forget that she herself was the first to smile at such
fantasies, telling us, moreover, that the true experience of
divine love is such that, once one has had it, one cannot
imagine there to be anything higher. Better yet: it is of the
essence of the unparalleled reality of this love that it gives
to each loved being the impression of being, as it were, the
sole object of the Father's love, so true is it that, in the end,
he loves us only in his Son, his only One![9]

---

[8] Attached to Vision XIII. See what Dom Porion says about it on page 40
of his preface to the *Poèmes*.

[9] There is something of this in all her outpourings on the love of God for
us as the true object of experience.

This leads us to say something about what we might call the principal sources of Hadewijch, whether named or not in the amusing document we have just mentioned. Saint John the Evangelist as well as Saint Augustine are naturally there in the first ranks because of the place and importance they attribute to love. Saint Bernard, of course, is fundamental as the one par excellence who introduced courtly imagery to represent what we might call the formation and growth of love in us. But it is very characteristic, as we will soon observe, that what interests her most in Bernard are in fact the fundamental theses of William of Saint Thierry, whose work was at that time confused with that of the Abbot of Clairvaux. And, let us add, she is in fact opposed to Bernard in that she does not admit absolutely the distinction between a human love for Christ the man and a divine love for Christ the God: for her, not only does the second pass through the first, but the first would be going the wrong way if it did not imply the second from the beginning, since there are not two Christs but a single Person in two natures. So it will be the same with any authentic love for him: it cannot for a single instant make an abstraction of his divine, incarnate Person.

We must also cite here Richard of Saint Victor, whose work she certainly knew well, for one of her letters incorporated an entire paragraph from it.[10]

But all these elements, in the work she has left us, seem as if recast into an intensely personal synthesis, which the *Visions* will illustrate, whose meaning is concretely explained in her *Letters* and becomes a song of praise in her *Poems*.

---

[10] This is Letter 10.

Exemplarism: Its Properly "Hadewigian" Meaning

In the *Visions* of Hadewijch, whether they are absorbed in the heavenly Jerusalem with its phalanxes of blessed spirits, the symbolic trees of the new paradise where it rises or simply in the figure of the invisible King who is its light, or whether, on the other hand, they apply to the decisive changes in her own spiritual progress, or whether they express simply, in varied forms, the constant soul of her mystical journey, what is remarkable from the very first is the fact that a single theme dominates them. And that is the theme of an incomparable love, of a love that belongs only to God. For that is the only love that gives all, that gives itself, that is only pure gift: that is, so to speak, the identity of God.

In fact, the God of whom it is always a question with her not only is love but is that love. Yet the effect, like the supreme testimony of the reality of such a divine love, is to make us love in that way: to love him, to love all that he loves, as he himself and he alone can love. Hence the terrible, apparently devastating demand of this love for whoever is its object. But this is simply the necessary path to lead us to the beatitude that is God himself.

Which is to say that we must be adapted to live in the mutual, constant, total, infinite renunciation of self that characterizes the three Divine Persons. For that, henceforth the principle of everything, is the action of the Father from whom all has proceeded. And it is also in that which the final unity of the whole Trinity consists, an essentially living unity.

But it is also our destiny! This divine unity wishes to consummate itself superlatively and to prolong itself, so to speak, in creation. For all that, it will introduce these creatures themselves, who carry the divine image, even to transcendent exchanges in which the Father, Son and Holy Spirit are but one, precisely because they are three, but those Three!

From this, Hadewijch derives the assurance that this nature of God cannot be known or, with even greater reason, be the object of our participation unless through and in the unheard-of experience in which the eternal Son, in becoming man, was to introduce us ourselves, all together but each one, for his part, irreplaceable. And from that, finally, that certitude, unshakable with Hadewijch and endlessly repeated, that it is only in uniting us, or rather in letting us unite, to this humanity of the God-made-man that we will be able to attain a true deification, which will consist in rendering him love for love: in loving as we are and have been from all eternity loved in him by the Father. In fact, through this response of love that is, in God, the Holy Spirit, the Son loves the Father in return; so, in becoming one with us, he wished only to carry us all along in this return of love to its source, which is its consummation as well. . . .

The *Letters* of Hadewijch, on the basis of this unique and extraordinary intuition, work both to elucidate it and to concretize its overall meaning, to justify at the same time as they illuminate the ways of its effective realization.

It will then appear that, for Hadewijch, the secret of this revelation, which is inseparable from its communication, lies in what the commentators usually call her "exemplarism".

It must be stressed, however, that she knew nothing of this term or, with greater reason, of all that it might suggest to those who apply it to her. In using it, in fact, one is obviously thinking not so much of the Platonic god as of the way the Neoplatonism of Plotinus and his disciples

understood him: which is to say, as the One par excellence,
who, however, manifests himself to us only in this *Nous*,
this eternal Thought, in which the Ideas of all being, of all
things are eternally conceived, "as if bursting with life", as
Plotinus himself tells us.[11] It is this life that will effectively
make the divine Soul its own by communicating it to the
whole world.

But, once again, all that this term "exemplarism" thus
evokes is only a parallel suggested by Dominican scholars
or Canons Regular, such as Eckhart or Ruusbroec, who later
explained or wanted to justify her doctrine intellectually in
the course of spreading it. She herself, despite all her learn-
ing, never seemed to have the slightest idea of it.

The only thing, in fact, that interests her in this regard is
the biblical word, and first of all as it appears in all clarity
from the Old Testament on—which is to say, a Word in
which God expresses himself, names himself, so to speak.
Yet, in eternally producing this Word who names him, he
conceives by the same stroke, wills and projects all his creatures into being. And such is eminently the case for this
creature in his image who is man, who is every man.

To be even more precise, it is this Word of the New Testament that Hadewijch has finally in view, this Word who
is the Son of God, his eternal Son, but through whom and
in whom he has created all. And with us all, this Son in
whom the Father was well pleased, with whom he is but a
single essence, but a single living nature, and on whom the
very Spirit of the Father rests as the Spirit of his filiation,
this Son returns, through the Spirit, with him, in him, all
his love to the Father.

[11] *Enneads* VI, 12 (in the Bréhier edition: volume VI, part 2, p. 83, lines
22 and 23).

In this whole biblical perspective, it seems to Hadewijch that, even before we existed concretely in our free individuality, we were all, in the living thought of the Father in his Son, eternally conceived and loved with him. So, eternally, we are predestined in him: all that we can, all that we should be, we will be only by identifying ourselves, through our free consent, which is itself the fruit of the divine Spirit, with what we were from all eternity in that living thought of the Father, which he projects into his Son and which returns to him in the Spirit as the thought of love, essentially loving as well as loved.

Nevertheless, there is no doubt that Hadewijch's reflection had been concentrated on this aspect of Christian revelation by a tradition that she undoubtedly drew from William of Saint Thierry. But he himself had received it through the twofold medium, it seems, of Pseudo-Dionysius and Scotus Eriugena, along with, between the latter two, the commentary that goes back, above all, to Maximus the Confessor.

This is, in fact, what this latter had expressed in a particularly felicitous way in saying that we are all, our most varied personalities and the historical destiny itself in which they will be fulfilled and will blossom, like so many *logoï* within the unique Logos and inseparable from him: from this expressed thought of the Father in which, from all eternity, in thinking himself, he thinks all that will ever be. It is thus that we are, all of us and each one of us, to recognize ourselves as eternally conceived, loved, willed such as we are to become in our concrete existence, through the Father in his Son.[12]

It is obviously to this eternal presence of ourselves in God,

----

[12] Cf. Lars Thunberg, *Microcosm and Mediator: The Theological Anthropology of Maximus the Confessor* (Copenhagen: Lund, 1965), 77 ff.

this presence to his thought, which is his eternal Word, that
some enigmatic-looking sentences, like the following in Letter 19, refer:

> Oh, may you grow according to that dignity which is yours
> and for which you were destined before time began! How
> can you endure it that God enjoys you in his essence, and
> you do not have enjoyment of him?

With even greater reason, it is the only possible explanation of Letter 18:

> Understand, too, the profound nature of your soul and the
> meaning of this word [soul, *siele*, in Flemish]. It is a being
> reached by the gaze of God and for whom God, in return,
> is visible [or better, transparent: *sinleec*].

It is, again, the presupposition of Letter 2:

> If, finally, you want to have what is yours [the existence to
> which we are destined], give yourself to God and become
> what he is.

Similarly, in Letter 6:

> You and I have not yet become what we are, have not yet
> caught hold of what we are, we tarry so far from what is
> ours.

And it is again in this perspective that Letter 22 exclaims:

> [All souls] thus love him according to his eternal nature, in
> which he will eternally satisfy all those who are to become
> God with God. . . . And he enjoys his wonder of infinite
> riches, in all the plenitude of glory, in all those who have
> been or will be or even who can be.

From this same perspective, she further says, in her Letter 6 already quoted:

If you want to return to the being in which God created you, you must, in all nobility, refuse no difficulty.

Still in the same letter:

And it is thus that he [Christ] has raised us and drawn us by his divine power and his human justice to our first dignity, giving us the freedom in which we had first been created and loved by God, confirming his call and our election such as he had foreseen from all eternity for our good.

In other words, the incarnate Word, as he includes us in himself ideally from all eternity, allows us through and in his Incarnation to become in ourselves, in time, what we were eternally in his divinity. This is what Letter 22 will expressly confirm by saying:

Everything is in him, from the beginning, as great as it will be without end.

A little farther on, she gives more of an explanation:

And since the power of the Father [let us understand here what is implied by the very unity of the divine essence, such as it is manifested fundamentally in his paternity] requires at every moment, with a terrifying demand, the unity in which he is sufficient to himself, he always comprises himself totally—yes! and all beings together, whatever their name: he includes them in his unity and calls all to the fruition of his being.

On the other hand, she stresses in her Letter 29:

But if I possess all this in love with my eternal being [that is, the intentional being that I have in God, in his Word, from all eternity], I do not yet possess it in fruition in my own being.

For, if lively faith, giving us over to the eternal love of
God, makes real in us what he willed for us in eternity in
willing us, it is only, Letter 19 explains:

the soul who is most untouched who is most like God. Ah!
May you grow according to that dignity that is yours and
to which you were destined before time began.

In the same sense, she said as early as her first letter:

Open the eyes of your heart to the light and see yourself
in God in holy truth.

This is confirmed by the first of her visions, in which
God says to her in Christ:

Remain in me from all eternity, entirely free and without
lapse.

The conclusion can be only these words, already quoted,
from Letter 19:

How can you endure it that God enjoys you in his essence,
and you do not have enjoyment of him?

As we see, in fact, it follows from this fundamental given
that there is in God a love of boundless generosity that, by
the very fact that we are eternally the objects of it, demands
that we love in him just as we have been loved by him.

This generosity in love is in fact what leads the soul, during its personal existence, to correspondence with what it is
in the idea that the Father gets of it in thinking and willing
it from all eternity in his Son.

So let us pass from the basic theme of exemplarity to the
central theme of the purity of love with which we must
love God in return.

We could quote the whole of Letter 6 on that:

The cross that we must bear with the Son of the living God is the sweet exile imposed on us because of just love, during which we must await with pure abandonment and holy desires the time of nuptials, when love will reveal itself, making its noble valor and power blaze forth on earth as they do in heaven. And from now on, it manifests itself so boldly to the soul in love that she is thrown outside herself: it ravishes her heart and senses, it makes her live and die from veritable love. . . .

The Generosity and Purity of Love

Letter 7 already announces the theme of God's love for us, which can be recognized only insofar as it leads us to the generosity, untouched by any egoism, that characterizes it:

> O Beloved, we must gain all things by means of themselves: strength with strength, understanding with understanding, love with love, all with all, like with like: only in this way do we fulfill what is required. Love suffices us and nothing else.

The following letter infers from this a twofold fear that must not leave the soul on her way to belonging to this divine love while being filled with it herself:

> In proportion as love grows between these two beings [God and the soul], a fear within the love also does not cease to increase. Or rather, it would be better to say a twofold fear. First of all, one fears not being worthy of so great a love, of never giving enough to grow into it, and this fear is perfectly noble. It, more than anything else, makes us advance, for it submits us totally to love. . . . The second fear is that love does not love us enough, for it binds us and distresses us so that we are overwhelmed beneath its weight and we truly seem to lack its help: we think we are the only ones

who love. This distrust is above an overly complacent faith,
a confidence that resigns itself before having attained pure
knowledge, content with the present moment. The high
challenge gives a new opening to the consciousness. . . .
[It is] such that it constantly maintains the fear either that
it does not love enough or that it is not loved.

In other words, the divine love itself purifies our love by
seeming to withhold itself from it, for it pushes us thereby
to love ever more purely in return, since we are never capable of meriting being loved like that.

This is what Letter 10 goes on to explain:

Desire for God is sometimes accompanied by a sensible
sweetness, but then it is still not entirely divine. . . . The
imperfect soul as well as the perfect can taste this plea-
sure and imagine itself to have a great love because it sa-
vors a sweetness, which is nevertheless not pure but still
mixed. And even if the sweetness is pure and wholly divine
—which requires subtle discernment—love should not be
measured by it but by the possession of the virtues and
charity. . . . Let us not claim our reward, let us do what
is up to us, and love will do what is up to it.

The whole of Letter 12 should be quoted on this subject.
Let us at least extract the essence of it:

All that we can think about God, or understand or imagine, is not God. For, if men could grasp him and conceive
of him with their faculties, God would be less than man,
and we would quickly stop loving him: so it is with superficial men whose love is so quickly spent.

In fact, the following letter tells us, the love of God is
limitless and so too, as a result, its demands. This is, therefore, the very reason that must convince us, says Letter 13,
that it will be satisfied only by a complete abandonment.

Thus the soul must exert all its strength toward the perfection of love—of love that is never to be appeased. For one does it in vain: a man can satisfy God in the eyes of those who see him, yet he is very far from satisfying love; he will not cease to feel its demands and its violent desires beyond all the goods acquired or possessed. One will only be able to please love by being deprived of all repose, whether this be in friends or strangers or in love itself. It is a terrifying demand of our life, in truth, that we must renounce even the satisfaction of love in order to satisfy love!

Letter 16 will sum up all that by simply saying:

Live nobly in hope and inviolable confidence that God will allow you to love him with this great love with which he loves himself, Three in One, the love by which he has eternally sufficed to himself and so suffices to himself always.

And Letter 18 can conclude:

Such is your debt, which you owe to God in all justice, according to the truth of your nature, as well as to the souls among whom you share his love: to love God alone with a perfectly simple intention and to have no other occupation but this one love, who has chosen us for himself alone.

This, obviously, can only be the supreme effect of what Christ did for us on the Cross, which raised him to the heavens, as Letter 19 will say:

When God and the blessed soul are united, then both will be exalted in all perfection and beauty. When the soul has nothing but God, when she has no other will but his simple will, when she is annihilated and wants all that God wants with the very will of God, when she is engulfed and reduced to nothing—then Christ is raised from the earth and draws all to himself: the soul becomes with him totally what he himself is.

Such is Hadewijch's last word on the manner in which
the love of God (that love which is absolutely proper to
him) must finally take its whole place in us through Jesus
Christ, or, rather, in Jesus Christ himself. We understand
henceforth that she will not hesitate to describe the union
that the love of God is to produce between him and us in
Christ as a union "without difference". There is not a trace
of pantheism in this: it is merely a matter of loving God as
we have been loved, by the wholly gratuitous infusion of
his own love. But this is also why she whom we call Hadewijch II will speak of a love "without why": to love as one
is loved—with such a love, quite obviously—has need of
no other justification than love itself!

And this is also what leads Hadewijch to employ repeat-
edly the word *Minne*, which means love, either to designate
Christ or to designate the soul itself, insofar as it is loved
by him and loving him in return.

This leads us to speak of what could be called Hadewijch's
doctrine on God and Christ, if there were the least trace in
her of that philosophico-theological inclination to which
Eckhart would give way and which was already pressing in
on Hadewijch II. But, at first, it is better to speak simply of
perspective.

Perspective on God and Christ

Hadewijch, in fact, is all too conscious of the obscurity of
faith in which what we can certainly call her experience
—mystical experience if there ever was, that is, eminently
mysterious—takes place to insist on translating it into any
metaphysics whatever. But, for all that, the faith from which
this experience proceeded is nonetheless a very defined faith.
The God of Jesus Christ, in fact, as the object of her faith,

is that God who is defined only by love, and very precisely the love that reveals itself as total, infinite generosity.

As for Christ—her Christ, we would be inclined to say if in seeing him that way she were doing anything but going straight to the heart of the gospel—he is the foremost incarnate object of that love; and, because of this, he is the second subject of it, before any creature, in his humanity as well as in his divinity from which it is inseparable.

First of all, it is very significant that, for Hadewijch, the nature, the essence of divinity, as indefinable as it certainly is for her, is revealed at this point in the Father, so that, to hear her talk, one might be tempted to think that the Father alone is God, properly speaking. In doing this, she is merely speaking like the first Fathers of the Church. Now, as Karl Rahner has observed well, for them, this simply means that, in the Father, one has, as it were, the revelation of divinity as an eternally flowing spring of that life that consists of love: the *agapē* of the New Testament. And this is also what she means.

Commenting on the Our Father in a trinitarian perspective, to which we will return in a moment, Letter 22 exclaims:

> We pray that his Kingdom might come, we [thus] enjoin the Unity in three Persons: we demand his power and his rich essence in our surrender to the Father. . . .

This is what her explanation a little farther on in the same letter will find, when she writes:

> And since the power of the Father requires at every moment, with a terrifying demand, the unity in which he is sufficient to himself, he always comprises himself totally —yes! and all beings together, whatever their name: he

includes them in his unity and calls all to the fruition of
his being.

Here, we once again find the theme of exemplarism, but
now raised by a wholly dynamic conception of grace, which
is itself dependent on an extraordinarily vivid vision of the
Trinity, into which, once again, that expression of the divine paternity can only lead. For the moment, let us be content to make our own the commentary of Dom Porion: this
power of the Father is of course the divine essence, since it
is fundamentally (we should say, in its source [*fontalement*])
revealed in the person whom the Greek Fathers did not fear
to describe as the "cause", which is to say, as the principle
of the Trinity itself and, thereby, of all being.

Here we have, not some abstract speculation, but the echo
of what the Christian God appears to be to the mystical soul.
This is what we are assured by the quotation drawn from
Letter 28, which it is legitimate to think is the personal rem-
iniscence of Hadewijch herself.

> Thus said someone in God: "My soul is completely torn
> to pieces by the violence of eternity, completely melted in
> the friendship of the Paternity, completely lavished with
> the grandeur of God: grandeur without measure, and the
> heart of my heart that is this wealth of God, my Lord, in
> [his] eternity!"

This is what she explains farther on in the same letter:

> God flows out of himself in holiness above all the saints in
> the Paternity, and from that he confers new riches, full of
> glory, on all his children. And because this is so, God can,
> today, tomorrow and always, give new riches, unknown
> and unheard-of by any but the Three Persons who heard
> of it from himself in eternity.

These words invite us to go on to what Hadewijch tells us about the Trinity. But one perceives already, since the Trinity is only the immanent fruit of that wholly generous love that is affirmed in the divine paternity, that to say in this sense that God is essentially Father presupposes a first Beloved eternally with the first Lover, a Beloved who, as such, loves as he does and with him, with that Love that is all his. This is the formula that brought fame to Richard of Saint Victor but that we now know he received from his master, Blessed Achard, later Bishop of Avranches. Although Hadewijch sometimes quotes Richard at length, she seems never to have taken up this formula. But it is clear that the latter applies no less to her spirituality than to the theology of the Victorines.

Letter 30, rather than a treatise on the Trinity, is in fact a series of lyrical variations on the way in which we are called to become, as she says, "God with God", drawn into the flow of the trinitarian life by the Son in whom we have been conceived from all eternity. The identification with our fallen humanity, which he has allowed, prepares, seeks and will accomplish, if we give ourselves to it in faith, this final identification of ourselves with our eternal principle.

The central part of the whole scope of this elevation must be quoted in its entirety:

> There are three things according to which one lives for Love, according to the Trinity here below and according to the Unity up above.
>
> First, reason makes one desire love and the satisfaction of that love through just works of perfect charity: one wants to be without fault and worthy of all perfection. In this way, one lives the Son of God.
>
> Next, to embrace at all hours the will of Love with a new zeal, to work in all virtue with an overflowing desire,

to enlighten all creatures according to their nature and the nobility that one recognizes in them, great or small, so that one accomplishes, in love and for its honor, the pure will of God: in this way, one lives the Holy Spirit.

In the third place, one finds oneself constrained by a gentle force to the constant practice of love, one receives the courage—henceforth happy and invincible—to face that state in which passion makes the Beloved grow in the being of the Loved One and to be penetrated by it in all things: to work with His hands, to walk with His feet, to hear with His ears where the divine voice never ceases to sound, to speak also through the mouth of the Beloved, in all truth, of counsel, of justice, of pure sweetness, of impartial consolation, of caution against evil—to appear like the Beloved without adornment of any kind, to live in nothing and for no one but in love and for the Beloved, to live like the Loved One with a single way of acting, a single thought, a single heart, to taste in him, as he in us, the inexpressible sweetness that is the fruit of his sufferings—oh yes! to feel nothing but heart to heart, with a single heart, a single sweet love, to have fruition, one in the other, of the fullness of love—to know without any doubt, with an ever more perfect certainty, that one is integrated into the Unity of Love: in this way, one lives the Father.

Profound thought is very evident here, in a vivid expression whose characteristics need not be taken rigidly, as if there were three different and successive moments in the Christian life, when it is actually a matter of a continuous interiorization of grace that, in the end, makes us fully realize what is at the root of all: the divine paternity extending to us in Christ through the Holy Spirit.

It is necessary to relate this text with that which opens Letter 17, a text that is at first glance still more enigmatic but is simply more filled with meaning. Dom Porion has summed up this letter very well by the title: "To act with the persons and to repose in the unity". It opens with a poem in paradoxical couplets, the second line of which almost seems to contradict the first:

> Be generous and zealous for every virtue,
> But do not apply yourself to any one virtue.
>
> Fail not with regard to a multitude of things,
> But perform no particular work.

And here is the explanation, first of all of the first couplet:

> These prohibitions that I give you are the very ones that God made me. I want, in my turn, to inform you of them because they belong in all truth to the perfection of love —because they are suited in a just and perfect way to the Deity. The attributes I have mentioned in fact describe [aspects of] the Divine Being. To "be prompt and zealous" is the character of the Holy Spirit, whereby he is a subsistent Person, but not to apply oneself "to any one virtue" is the nature of the Father; he is thereby Father without distinctions. This giving and this keeping back is the very Deity and the whole nature of Love.

And now, here is the explanation of the second couplet:

> The first line describes the power of the Father, whereby he is the all-powerful God: and the second describes his just will, by which he accomplishes his sovereign and secret works in the heart of deep darkness, unknown and hidden to all who are below that pure unity of the Deity.

These texts give rise to a whole series of observations.

The first is the use that Hadewijch has already made of the word "Deity", which is also found particularly in Meister Eckhart (*Gottheit*), who contrasts it with "God" (*Gott*), by which is understood the Three Divine Persons, while Deity represents their transcendent unity.[13]

Yet, in reading these texts of Hadewijch, it is immediately clear that, at least for her, it is not at all a question of a pure unity of Plotinian style, which would go beyond, surpass, in its eternal immobility, the level of the Persons. These texts, in fact, exclaim exactly the contrary. For Hadewijch, the Deity, its Unity or, as she also says, its Repose, which belongs fundamentally to the Father, to whom all must return just as from whom all has proceeded, is the constant stream, or, better said, the ebb that is inseparable from the unceasing flow of the unique Love: that Love that not only unites them but constitutes them in a living unity.

A second point to note here is the ever-synthetic, or, better still, the immediately one way in which she considers Christ: that is to say, in his humanity, but always insofar as his Divine Person involves him in this eternal current of the Deity. And it is precisely in this that, by uniting himself to us in his redemptive Incarnation, he wishes to make us participate. He will do so effectively to the degree in which we surrender ourselves, without more resistance, to this flow of divine love that reaches us in the encounter with him. That is to say, insofar as we abandon ourselves to the ebb of this love, which, through the Spirit, in Christ, will plunge us, not in order to annihilate us, but in order to accomplish everything in us, up to the very heart of the Father.

It is in this ultimate perspective that Hadewijch does not fear to say that the Son himself, as he was begotten of the Father from all eternity, is "engulfed", literally, by this ebb of the distinctive love of the Father that this Spirit of filiation that reposes on him specifically is. Let us note again: this is

---

[13] See below, 63ff.

also what explains how this "repose" of unity, in the Deity, will also be called paradoxically by Hadewijch a "tempest"!

All this is going to be expressed, in a rather confused manner, as if possessed by enthusiasm, in what follows in the same letter quoted above, passing on to the commentary on the third couplet. The latter tells us:

Have good will and compassion for every need,
But take nothing under your protection.

Here, then, is the final explanation:

[Those of whom we have just spoken] are below the Unity, while serving the Persons as is fitting for each one, in all fidelity, as I say in the first line [of each couplet]: "Be generous and zealous for every virtue"—"Do not neglect any work"—"Have good will and compassion for every need." That, in truth, seems the finest life that could be led here on earth: I have not ceased to recommend it above all to you; as you know, I first of all lived it in devotion and in works, in all nobility, until the day when it was forbidden me.

The other three lines [the second of each couplet] express the perfection of union and love: love, in all justice, attends to itself and to nothing else—a single being, a single charity! Oh, what Essence is as terrifying as that which engulfs so much hatred and so much love into the unity of its nature!

Have good will and compassion for every need corresponds to the Son insofar as a distinct Divine Person: such as he was and such as his work was in all beauty:—*but take nothing under your protection*, [here] again, it is the Father who engulfs the Son: such is always his work, whose immensity frightens us.

That is the unity, beautiful above all things, of the Deity's love: it is so just, with the justices of love, that it absorbs the zeal and the humanity and the power, which would leave no need unmet. . . .

Yet, how are we to understand this excess? This is what leads us to see how Hadewijch (whom Ruusbroec will follow particularly closely on this point) understands the relation between practical charity and the contemplation we call mystical.

Flow of Love of Neighbor and Ebb of Love into God

First of all, it is the very Incarnation of the Son of God that shows us that we cannot love God as he wishes to be loved without beginning by loving our neighbors as he has loved them.

Such is the whole lesson of Letter 15:

> Since [Christ] is the way, we must follow in his footsteps: as he worked, as he burned interiorly with charity and as he translated that exteriorly into works of virtue toward strangers and friends, as he commanded men to love God with all their heart, all their soul, all their strength, and never to forget this either while waking or sleeping. And see how he did this himself, even though he was God: how he gave all and left all for true love, the love of the Father, and through compassion toward men. He lived in an ever-vigilant charity, giving all his heart, all his soul and all his strength to love. Such is the way that Jesus shows us and that he himself is: the way he followed and in which is found eternal life, the fruition in the glory and truth of his Father.

In other words, it is the very love we witness here below toward our neighbors that will prepare us for that repose of love into which we will enter, as Christ entered it at the end of his earthly life.

> For [Letter 3 tells us already] brotherly love follows the order indicated in the charity of Jesus. . . . In this way, we touch God truly on the side where he cannot defend himself, for we do so with his own work, with the will of his Father whose commandment he fulfilled. And thus Love reveals many a marvel to our understanding, many a heavenly truth to our admiration.

Just what revelation is in question here, Letter 12 tells us very precisely:

> Those who are on fire with the concern to please God are, like him, eternal and unfathomable. For their conversation is in the heavens and their soul follows everywhere the Beloved, who is of infinite depths. . . .
>
> [So] I earnestly entreat you and I beg you by the true fidelity that is God himself to make haste to love and to help us to make God loved: that is what I ask you first and above all. At all hours think of the goodness of God and grieve to know that it remains outside our grasp, while he has perfect fruition of it, that we are exiled far from it, while he himself and his friends, in a mutual interpenetration, enjoy the superabundance of this goodness, flow into it and flow back out again in all fullness. Oh, this God in truth: he cannot be known by any sort of effort if just love does not reveal him! It is love alone that attracts him to us and makes us feel intimately who our God is: we would have no other way of knowing him.

This pivotal text will be the seed for Ruusbroec's developments on the inevitable alternation here below between service of the neighbor, in which the flow of divine love toward the self is manifested, and contemplation, in which its ebb toward its source is affirmed.

In eternity, however, there will no longer be such an alternation: it will be for us human persons as it is for the divine: it is with a single impulse that all the elect now being gathered together, and having attained perfection, will all love each other as God loves them by loving him in return.

Insofar as love is made perfect in us, we have some foretaste of this consummation in Unity.

This is what Letter 17 implies in one of its final paragraphs:

> While one is seeking love and is in its service, one must do all for its glory, for during all this time, one is human and remains in need: we must act generously in all things, love our neighbor personally, serve him and show compassion on his afflictions, for we feel lack and need everywhere. But, in the divine fruition, one becomes God, powerful and just. Then, will, work and power will be equally just. These three are [as it were] the Three Persons in one God.

One will note this affirmation, undoubtedly the most decisive from the pen of Hadewijch, of what the Greek Fathers called our "divinization". But, as we have understood it to be telling us all along: if it is a matter of becoming "God with God", this is possible only in Jesus Christ, dead and resurrected, through his Spirit descended upon us because of his own Ascension to the Father.

Nevertheless, in the final analysis, the greatest mystery, for our Beguine as well as for Saint Paul, who was to write the Letter to the Ephesians, it is not so much the mystery of ourselves in Christ: it is, first and above all, this mystery of the Christian God himself, whose eternal repose is also life, movement itself, because it is a life made of the Love that is only gift.

This is the summit to which Letter 22 leads us and with which it leaves us, a letter whose riches will never be exhausted:

> The [last] point: that God is in everything and uncircumscribed, must be understood in the eternal fruition of himself, in the dark power of the Father, in the wonder of his love of self, in the clear, upwelling flow of the Holy Spirit. God is thus the unitive storm that condemns or blesses each thing according to its worth. He has fruition of himself in this depth, according to the glory of the Being that he is in himself.

The Birth of Christ in Us

We must return once again to the final characteristic of Hadewigian spirituality, which will take on capital importance in Eckhart's spirituality and which also goes back to the ancient Fathers. This is the idea that, as Christ is born of his Father from all eternity, as he is born in Bethlehem of the Virgin Mary, so must he finally be born in us.

Yet, with Hadewijch, in a typically feminine fashion, this theme assumes a particular meaning.

With the Fathers, to begin with Origen, and also for Eckhart, after her, this is a way of expressing our incorporation, our identification with Christ. But, with Hadewijch, it is much more a matter of identification with Mary: the faithful soul is called to conceive and give rebirth to Christ from her own humanity. We will find something of this once again in Tauler.

This is what the fourteenth in the second series of her poems teaches.

. . . Provided one sink low in humility,
Lower still than any man,
The greatness of Love will thereby come to us.
Thus humbling yourself lower than all,
You would obtain perfect love.
It was in this way that Mary attracted God,
He would do the same
For love as humble.
He could not refuse one his greatness,
Who would as such receive him, carry him
As a child is formed in its Mother. . . .
So the soul receives as Mary did,
More humble even than obedient,
To be the Servant of the Lord.

As the reader will have observed, this is the first poem
we have quoted from Hadewijch. In fact, throughout this
entire sketch, we have concentrated on the explanation that
she herself gives of her experience, and, in general, this is
put forward by her letters.

Yet reading the letters is or should be only a preface to
the poems, whose object is to urge us, indeed, to propel us
in that quest for divine Love by that very love that faith in
Christ awakens in us. Unfortunately, like all poems, hers
lose much in translation. We could not, all the same, conclude this chapter without quoting at the very least one of
the translations given by Mother Columba Hart. It is drawn
from one of the many examples in Hadewijch of a spring
aubade, so familiar to courtly literature. And it offers the
advantage of leading us straight to the essence: the acceptance without reservation of all that the easy yoke, the light
burden of the gospel imply—which is nothing other than
that "love of God poured into our hearts by the Holy Spirit
who has been given to us", as the apostle Saint Paul says.

Now is born the noble season
That will bring us *flowers in the land.*
So it is for the noble hearts, chosen
To bear the yoke, the chains of Love:
Fidelity ever blossoms in their hands
With flowers and fruits of nobleness;
Among them the word is experienced by fidelity;
   Among them Love remains constant
Through one friendship, intimately united
   In the highest counsel of Love.

My yoke is sweet, my burden light,
Says the Lover of Love himself
This word he had beautifully expressed in Love;
Outside of Love one cannot experience its truth,
To my way of thinking.
So for them the light burden is heavy,
And they suffer many an alien fear
   Since they live outside of Love;
For the servants' law is fear,
   But love is the law of sons.

What is this light burden of Love
And this sweet-tasting yoke?
It is the noble load of the spirit,
With which Love touches the loving soul
And unites it to her with one will
And with one being, without reversal.
The depth of desire pours out continually,
   And Love drinks all that outpouring.
The debt Love summons love to pay
   Is more than any mind can grasp.

No heart or mind could ever guess
How anyone looks with love on his Beloved

When Love has heavily burdened him with love;
He will not waste an instant's time
Until he passes with love through all,
To gaze with fidelity on true Love;
For all his judgments must be
    Read in Love's countenance.
And there he sees clear truth without illusion
    In many a sweet pain.

He sees in clarity that one who loves
Must live with full truth;
When he then understands with truth
That he does too little for Love,
His noble mind is forcibly stirred;
For in Love's face he learns fully
How love shall practice love;
    And this judgment sweetens his pain
And makes him give all for all,
    In order to content Love.

To those who give themselves thus to content Love,
What great wonders shall happen!
With love they shall cleave in oneness to Love,
And with love they shall contemplate all Love—
Drawing, through her secret veins,
On the channel where Love gives all love,
And inebriates all her drunken friends with love
    In amazement before her violence:
This remains wholly hidden from aliens,
    But well known to the wise.

To all who desire love, may God grant
That they be so prepared for Love
That they all live on her riches

Until, after themselves becoming Love, they draw Love
    into themselves
So that nothing evil, on the part of cruel aliens,
Can befall them more; but they shall live free
To cry: *I am all Love's, and Love is all mine!*
    What can now disturb them?
For under Love's power stand
    The sun, moon, and stars![14]

[14] Mother Columba Hart, O.S.B., *Hadewijch: The Complete Works*, 157–59. Rereading Origen, we find a unique text in which assimilation to Mary (in relation to the theme of the birth of Christ in us) is already found: *Second Homily on the Song of Songs*, 6 (cf. *Tenth Homily on Exodus*, 3–4).

II

FROM HADEWIJCH TO
ECKHART AND RUUSBROEC

From Hadewijch I to Hadewijch II

If it were necessary to characterize one fundamental trait of Hadewijch's spiritual work, one might say that it is the expression of a spirituality arising wholly from the traditional Catholic Faith, but one in which abstract speculation, from dogma given over to a philosophico-theological analysis, has no part. All that is most profound in what she tells us about Christ and the soul, about the entrance of the latter into what comprises the living unity of the Trinity itself, through consummation of a union, in lively faith, with the Son of God made man, is distinguished, at a time when the great Scholastic syntheses were being constructed, by the fact that she seems to have been unaware even of their existence. For her, all that she says remains in the sole perspective of the Love that God is, according to Saint John. That love itself, such as she interprets it, sings it, proposes it, encourages us to surrender ourselves to it, as she does, consists of a simple deepening of the word of Jesus that Saint Paul conveys to us in the eighth chapter of the Second Letter to the Corinthians: "It is more blessed to give than to receive." In a word, it is simply, but in its lived fullness, New Testament *agapē*.

Thus, at a time when even the most orthodox Catholic thinkers (and, well before the end of the century, this will

be all the more true of those who were less orthodox) were
tending to develop theology into metaphysical speculation,
we note absolutely nothing of this in her, as theological as
her spirituality may be in its foundation. The theology that
is certainly, as it were, implied in her spirituality is not sep-
arate from it, and one can even say that, just as was true
of the greatest Fathers of the ancient Church, it cannot be
detached from it. It is a theology that remains spiritual in
the whole of its substance. If Evagrius' saying—that "theologian" and "man of prayer" are two synonymous expressions—ever had meaning, it is indeed the case with Hadewijch. Nothing is more characteristic in this regard than
the way in which she uses the theme of exemplarism, her
most fundamental theme, yet taken back to a theological
tradition wholly charged with philosophical reminiscences.
Once again, it is very revealing that she never uses the word
itself or any related term.

As close as the bond may be and as profound as the relationship may appear between Hadewijch and her successor, Hadewijch II, as she is called (the supposition that they
might be two different personalities never crossed the mind
of Ruusbroec or his disciple John Leeuwen), it is with Hadewijch II that we hear the first, I will not say discordant, note
but surely one conveying the passage to another register, that
of pure speculation, even if it is true that here again the meditation with a metaphysical turn of phrase, proceeding from
prayer, immediately returns to it.

What do we find that is new in this second Hadewijch
with respect to her precursor? Dom Porion has noted nakedness, the pure unencumbered state of mind, the simple substance of our being, the flash of soul, the mirror in us that

is always ready to reflect the Divinity, union without mode or intermediary.[1]

Let us stress, nevertheless, that the first concern remains very spiritual, and the intellectuality that passes even into her poems (those of her precursor were even more untouched by it than her letters) takes nothing away from the freshness, the youth, which is as striking in her verses as in those of the first Hadewijch.

Be that as it may, all these themes have always been so well known as belonging essentially to the spirituality of Meister Eckhart, which is so speculative in its expressions, that it seems obvious that the second Hadewijch was definitely later than the Rhenish master.

This is so true that one need do no more than quote the last of her poems to be disposed to believe it: even though it employs only one of the themes we are used to thinking of as "Eckhartian" (here, the nakedness of the divine essence, demanding emptiness of the soul that wants to be united with it), the entire atmosphere is one in which the preaching of the enigmatic Dominican breathes forth:

> Salvation! foremost source in ourselves
> that gives us noble, heavenly knowledge
> and ever-renewed nourishment of love,
> and frees your intelligence in us
> from any accident coming from outside.
>
> The unity of naked truth,
> abolishing all reasons,
> holds me in this emptiness

---

[1] J.-B. Porion, *Hadewijch d'Anvers, Poèmes des béguines*, 45.

and adapts me to the simple nature
of the eternity of the eternal Essence.

Here I am stripped of all reasons.
Those who have never understood Scripture
would not know how to explain with reasoning
what I have found in myself
—without milieu, without veil—above the words.[2]

Position of Meister Eckhart

That this Hadewijch II thus depends on Eckhart, while remaining very close to our Hadewijch I, is nevertheless what
Father Ampe and Father Mens, as difficult as it seems for
them to reject it, are beginning themselves to believe uncertain, while Father Van Mierlo, for his part, as well as Dom
Porion, have scarcely any doubt about her anteriority.

On the one hand, in fact, all the themes that have just
been brought forward, which are as typical of Eckhart as
their constellation seems to be, are nevertheless found, al-
beit in scattered order, in the spiritual literature of the North,
particularly in the Netherlands, well before Eckhart; and a
striking example of it, regarding the exaltation of poverty,
will even be found in an Italian *lauda* attributed to Jacopone
da Todi!

And, on the other hand, experts of the Flemish language
and of its evolution deem it impossible to date the poems
of Hadewijch II later than the second half of the thirteenth
century.[3]

[2] Ibid., 182.
[3] Ibid., 47 ff.

Be that as it may, it is not our purpose here to deal with Eckhart or Ruusbroec or even Saint John of the Cross in themselves. What we would like to attempt in this chapter is simply to show how Eckhart in particular has brilliantly interpreted, through a combination that is typical of Rhenish theology of the fourteenth century, a spiritual experience and doctrine whose first expression and foremost example go back to the first and, we would say, the great Hadewijch. The combination of which we speak is the synthesis (which is still very personal even though prepared for by a whole generation of German thinkers) that Eckhart makes between a theology with a Thomistic base and contributions that are still more Neoplatonic than Platonic, picked up from Plotinus but also from Proclus.[4] In Ruusbroec, as we will see next, the systematic elaboration of Hadewijch's doctrine is no less constructive, but what it owes to Rhenish Neoplatonism is not as clear.

This, however, in no way signifies that Meister Eckhart is not himself a spiritual master, and a very great spiritual master, in his own right. But, if Father E. H. Weber has been able to demonstrate authoritatively that he is a mystic because a theologian,[5] we would be inclined to emphasize even more that he is the very personal theologian he is without any doubt only because of his mystical experience. Yet, the latter was developed not only along the lines but as an evident direct descendant of what we can call the Hadewigian tradition. To our mind, we have here a typical case of a masculine elucidation of intuitions that were at first feminine, an elucidation that does not clarify and justify them without

[4] A. de Libera, *Introduction à la mystique rhénane*, 30.
[5] E. H. Weber, *Mystique parce que théologien: Maître Eckhart*, 730ff. of the special issue of *Vie spirituelle* on *Les Mystiques rhenans* (November 1982).

some risk of preparing the way for their evaporation into theologoumena of a more or less dangerous abstraction.

We are rather well informed about Eckhart's personality, his biography, particularly about his formation and his activities.[6] Our documentation is lacking only about the exact time and circumstances of his death as well as about certain details of his process.

Born around 1260 in one of the two villages of Thuringia that bear the name of Hochheim (we still do not know which), he must have entered the Dominican monastery of Erfurt at an early age. Having studied first at the *studium generale* of his order, founded in Cologne by Albert the Great, then in Paris, he soon became the prior of the monastery where he had been received. Later, he was provincial of Saxony, which is to say that he had under his authority around half of the monasteries in Germany. In 1307, the general chapter that had been convened at Strasbourg entrusted to him the charge of a vicariate over Bohemia, with full authority for reform there as needed. He thus had responsibility for forty-seven monasteries of men and nine of women. Not only did that lead to the founding of three new monasteries, but his visits were already the occasion of preaching that very quickly became immensely popular, as evidenced by the numerous notes of sermons taken down by listeners that have endured to this day. In 1311, at the general chapter held in Naples, there was a question of mak-

---

[6] For all that concerns Eckhart's biography and the critical edition of his works, refer to the excellent introduction by Jeanne Ancelet-Hustache to her translations of both the *Traites* (Paris, 1971) and the *Sermons* (Paris, 1974–1979). See also the introduction of Bernard McGinn to the two volumes of English translations that he has made (the first in collaboration with Edmund Colledge), in 1981 and 1986. (*Meister Eckhart: The Essential Sermons, Commentaries, Treatises and Defense* [Mahwah, N.J.: Paulist Press, 1981].)

ing him master general. But, in the end, they preferred to send him again to Paris to teach for a second time.

In 1314, however, having been made vicar general of the whole order, with jurisdiction over the convents of women, he took up permanent residence in Strasbourg and was soon teaching again, but in Cologne. It was at this time that things were going to deteriorate.

The Archbishop of Cologne, Heinrich von Virneberg, like many other prelates, was not overly fond of the Dominicans, whose popularity attracted the gifts of the faithful—leaving so much the less to fall into the episcopal treasuries! Added to that was the unrest caused by heretical, pantheistic Beguines, who appeared to have drawn some of their boldest expressions from the mysticism of the Meister. Further repercussions cropped up as a result of the conflict between Louis de Bavière, pretender to the Empire, and John XXII (the Avignon pope against whom he would create an anti-pope)! It seems very likely that the Archbishop had also played on a dissension between the Dominicans of Cologne, where Eckhart had used his authority against two rebels, in order to attack him.

All the same, the prelate launched an accusation of heresy against Eckhart and named a commission of two members in order to investigate it. The fact that, with his inquisitor, Master Reyner, Heinrich named Peter of Estate, a Franciscan (at a time when the latter were opposed to the Dominicans on both the political as well as the doctrinal level), is enough to make the impartiality of his intervention doubtful. The two investigators drew up two series of offensive propositions in succession. Eckhart, while protesting his twofold exemption (as Dominican and as Parisian master, he could be judged only by his peers), defended the indicted articles, declaring: "I can be mistaken; I cannot be heretical, for an error is a matter of intelligence; heresy depends on the will." Three more lists, which we do not have, seem to have been produced, while Meister Eckhart appealed to the Avignon Pope and pronounced, from his seat in Cologne, a solemn declaration of fidelity to the teaching of the Church.

It was only in 1935 that the report of the papal commission was discovered. Of the more than one hundred propositions indicted in Cologne, the judges in Avignon retained only twenty-eight. For each one, they give the motives for condemning it, the response of the accused and their counter to the latter.

It is clear that at this time, Eckhart, undoubtedly exhausted, discouraged, probably sick, was no longer in full possession of his abilities. His defense is uncertain, inarticulate. As for the Avignon judges, not only did they retain, in order to sift through them, only twenty-eight propositions, but, among these latter themselves, they recognized that the accused declared two of them to be inauthentic, while besides these two there were only fifteen that might properly be considered heretical; the others, as offensive as they might appear, admitted of an orthodox sense, "with many explanations and complements". The simple fact that the bull of John XXII, *In agro dominico*, informing the Archbishop of Cologne of this limited condemnation, specifies that the condemned, "at the end of his life . . . revoked and deplored the twenty-six [condemned] articles that he had admitted having preached and also whatever others he may have written or taught . . . insofar as they might engender in the mind of the faithful a heretical opinion or one that is erroneous and hostile to the true Faith", informs us, first of all, that Eckhart had died before its publication, dated March 27, 1329. But it also implies that he did not believe it

necessary to abandon, and that he was apparently not forced
to reject, any of the indicted propositions, *in the sense in which
he himself had expressed them.*

This seems corroborated by the fact that one of the most
distinguished of his judges, Cardinal Jean Fournier (who
succeeded John XXII under the name of Benedict XII), has
left us, in a written document, the testimony of his dissatisfaction with the method followed in this proceeding, as in
others of the same period: that is, the fact that the propositions were examined in the abstract (*ut sonant*) without
reference to the context in which they had been inserted.
To this central observation must be added the fact that the
Avignon judges themselves had only an inadequate knowledge of tradition and did not take into account the fact that
several of the rejected formulas are found either in Saint
Augustine himself or in other Fathers.

In a general way, in the following generations, not only
the disciples faithful to Eckhart, who were themselves always seriously suspected of error, like Tauler and Suso, but
an independent authority as considerable as Cardinal Nicolas
of Cusa, in the fifteenth century, would remain persuaded
of the fundamental orthodoxy of the disputed master.

In reality, the appearance of either pantheism or quietism
that some thought to find in Eckhart, at a time when some
undoubtedly heretical mystics from the Beghard circles were
claiming him as their authority, covered nothing that was not
already in Hadewijch or would not be found equally again
in the Spanish mystics of the sixteenth century of whom
we will soon speak and whom the Holy See was not only
to canonize but to proclaim Doctors of the Church.

Yet, there is one point in Eckhart's teaching that con-
tinues to be surrounded by ambiguity. Curiously enough,
his Avignon censors seem scarcely to have noticed it: they

barely touch it in passing in their propositions 23 and 24, on the point that there might not be any real distinction in God.

We would like to speak of what becomes in Eckhart an opposition that Hadewijch had already observed: between the Persons taken separately from each other and what she too, already, calls "the Deity". But, for her, it is clear that this term designates, as we have seen, the very life of the Persons, beginning with the Father. In other words, it is only this love that, in producing the Son equal to the Father, makes him come back in the Spirit to the Father in order to be "engulfed" there, as she says.

In Eckhart, the opposition seems to harden: it becomes explicitly an opposition between "God" (all that is personal in the Divinity) and this Deity. But especially, with his constant use of a dialectic between the multiple and the one (sole divine in the fullness of that sense) that goes back to Proclus and Plotinus, to read many texts of the Meister in isolation, it could seem, and in fact many modern readers still believe, that he wishes to place above the Persons an impersonal Essence that one would have to reach in order to attain in God what is fundamentally proper to him.

This is what Reiner Schürmann, for example, grants as self-evident in his *Maître Eckhart ou la joie errante*.[7] For him, this amounts to saying that Eckhart's mystical experience has nothing in it to distinguish it from the experiences of, among others, Zen Buddhism. If this were so, obviously, Eckhart would be justifying a position that seems to hypnotize Father Le Saux and, it would appear, is indeed the

---

[7] Paris, 1972. Cf. Bede Griffiths, *Expérience chrétienne, mystique, hindoue* (Paris, 1985), and Henri Le Saux, *La Montée au fond du coeur: Le journal intime de moine chrétien-sannyasi hindou* (Paris: OEIL, 1986).

one that Father Bede Griffiths makes his own: The entire Christian Faith, belief in the Trinity and the redemptive Incarnation, merely constitute a propaedeutic to be used by the West in order to prepare for a supreme religious experience, transcending all of that, something that the contemplatives of India attain, for their part, without any need to pass through this intermediary!

This is what modern Buddhists, on their side, like the propagator of modernized Zen, Dr. Daisetz T. Suzuki, or Shizuteru Ueda consider evident.[8]

In fact, despite his aversion to any dogmatic form of Christianity, Rudolf Otto, as early as 1926, thanks to the rigor and perfect honesty of his phenomenological analyses, dissipated these illusions. His very keen comparison between what is called the Hindu "mysticism" of Sankara and that of Eckhart, departing from the apparent alliance in the two spiritual masters of images borrowed either from the fusion of substances or from a relation of personal love like that between a man and a woman, results in an affidavit of total heterogeneity. In Eckhart, he says, it is the union of Persons that is fundamental, while in Sankara, it is the unity of substance.[9]

More recently, an American contemporary, the excellent specialist in Eckhartian studies, Bernard McGinn, in his study: "The God beyond God: Theology and Mysticism in the Thought of Meister Eckhart", has definitively invalidated this kind of confusion.

---

[8] Cf. D. T. Suzuki, *Mysticism, Christian and Buddhist* (Westport, Conn.: Greenwood Press, 1976), and S. Ueda, *Meister Eckhart und der Zen Buddhism* (Gütersloh, 1966).

[9] Rudolf Otto, *Mysticism East and West: A Comparative Analysis of the Nature of Mysticism* (New York: Macmillan, 1970).

Thus, he writes:

> If we wish to be true to Eckhart, we must admit the ground-
> ing priority of the hidden Unity of the Godhead, abso-
> lute and undetermined *esse*, the God beyond God, over the
> Trinity of Persons. But if we stop there and refuse to rec-
> ognize that the *unum* dialectically demands expression as
> a Trinity of Persons we shall also be false to the Meis-
> ter. A text from vernacular sermon 10 puts the dialectical
> relation in a nutshell: "Distinction comes from Absolute
> Unity, that is, the distinction in the Trinity. Absolute Unity
> is the distinction and distinction is the Unity. The greater
> the distinction, the greater the Unity, for that is the distinc-
> tion without distinction."[10]

And, as the rest of the text moves from this to that other
distinction in the Unity, which is produced by created persons, whose very distinction from their Creator prepares the
way for their reunion with him in the grace of adoption,
McGinn rightly concludes, in words borrowed entirely from
Eckhart:

> The divine inner *bullitio*, the emanation of the Persons of
> the Trinity, provides the exemplary model for all *ebullitio*,
> that is, all efficient and final causality, either creation on
> the part of God or the making of one thing from another
> by secondary causes. In fine, the divine unity is prior to
> the Trinity as the hidden ground of the *bullitio* of Father,
> Son, and Holy Spirit, but it can never be considered alone
> as standing in some sort of frozen immobility, nor could
> such a desert without bloom be the goal of the soul's jour-
> ney. The *unum* is not negation, but negation of negation,
> the *sum qui sum* ("I am that I am") of Exodus 3:14 that sig-
> nifies the conversion of the ground of *esse* upon itself.[11]

[10] *Journal of Religion* (University of Chicago), vol. 61:13–14.
[11] Ibid., 14–15.

Let us add to this significant quotation and its commentary a remark that may be still more important, made by the same author a little earlier:

> The God/Godhead distinction as found in the German works is by no means uniform. Frequently, it is used to distinguish the Father as the source of the other Persons of the Trinity, as when we read: "The Father is an origin of the Godhead for he comprehends himself in himself" [in sermon 15, volume 1 of the *Deutsche Werken*, p. 252, lines 2 and 13].[12]

McGinn quotes still other texts moving in the same direction and observes that Bonaventure was already expressing himself in the same way.

From all this, it is clear that Eckhart has in fact the same view of things as Hadewijch: very far from presuming to transcend the Trinity, he wishes to lead us to an idea of the Trinity that is dynamic rather than static.

Here we have, in different terms, what the Greek Fathers mean in speaking of the *perichoresis* of the Divine Persons (which the Latin would translate, not as *circumsessio*, which is precisely static, but as the dynamic *circumcessio*: not the mere presence of one in the other, but the impulse of the one toward the other). And this is what Pope Dionysius wrote to his namesake Dionysius of Alexandria: that the Trinity, which opens out from the Father into the Son, is summed up in the Father by the Spirit.[13] In another way, Augustine tried to express the same sentiment in describing the Divine Persons as *relationes substantiae*: relations by which, in which, they subsist, the one in the other, the one for the other.[14]

---

[12] Ibid., pp. 11–12.

[13] Cf. Saint Athanasius, *De Sententia Dionysi*, par. 17 (PG 25, col. 505A).

[14] *De Trinitate*, book V, chap. 11.

The whole difference on this point between Eckhart and Hadewijch stems from the fact that he has tried through speculation to elucidate what he had received spiritually from the Hadewigian tradition and to make it his own through an experience no less personal than that of Hadewijch herself.

One can only wonder whether recourse to Neoplatonism and its dialectic of the one and the multiple was fortuitous in translating the biblical conception of God. Pseudo-Dionysius, who was himself better informed than anyone, had taken hold of it. As Vladimir Lossky has seen very well: he made use of it only in pushing it still farther: in applying the idea, launched by Gregory of Nazianzen, that God is as well beyond the one as he is beyond the multiple![15]

McGinn, however, in another study, makes a remark scarcely less important than the preceding:

> Eckhart claims that Absolute Unity or the One is proper to the intellect alone, because all material beings are composed of matter and form, and immaterial beings are also composed, at least of *essentia* and *esse*, and more radically of *esse* and *intelligere*. God alone lacks these compositions because he is *one*, he is pure *esse* and totally *intellectus*.[16]

The Eckhartian insistence on the primacy in God of *intelligere* over *esse* itself will certainly appear more satisfactory. If Lonergan is not mistaken, it is to Saint Thomas Aquinas that we must go back for the origin of this affirmation.[17] In any case, there is no doubt that his *De Veritate* presupposes in

[15] *Oratio: Theologia tertia*, par. 2 (PG 36, cols. 74ff.).

[16] "Meister Eckhart on God as Absolute Unity", in the collected volume *Neoplatonism and Christian Thought*, edited by Dominic O'Meara (Albany: New York State University Press, 1982), 136.

[17] See B. Lonergan, *Verbum: Word and Idea in Aquinas* (Notre Dame, Ind.: University of Notre Dame Press, 1967).

God himself, from all eternity, the knowledge of all created beings, as included in the knowledge that he has of himself in his own Word. And, as we have stressed above, Saint Maximus the Confessor was already understanding thereby a knowledge, as mysterious as it might be, of all personal beings not only in their individuality but in the whole development that was to lead them, according to eternal predestination, to live from his own life. This is the same sentiment that inspired Eckhart in his use of the term *bullitio*, applied to the production of the Divine Persons, completed by *ebullitio*, for that of creatures, a singular transposition of the very notions borrowed from Neoplatonism in order to render them susceptible of a Christian sense. In fact, the One, for Plotinus and his successors, just like the Aristotelian God, "thought by the thought", could know nothing (insofar as one can consider him as knowing) except himself and him alone. It is the Nous, the Thought that proceeds directly from it, that has the task of being the receptacle of the ideas of all things and of all particular being. But Plotinus insists that this very thought is "boiling with life". Yet, even considered as such, it represents a first degradation with respect to the One and prepares the way for that of the Soul, which will follow.[18]

For Eckhart, on the contrary, it is proper to the divine Essence, manifested fundamentally in the Father, to present this *bullitio*, in virtue of which it is realized in the Persons. And it is as if through a new development of this divine life outside itself that it will be prolonged, through a first and confounding gratuity, in the *ebullitio* that will constitute creation, called, through an even more confounding grace

----

[18] Sixth *Ennead*, 12, in the Bréhier edition, p. 83 of the second part of vol. 6, lines 22 and 23.

—but for all that the supreme revelation of what this God is
—to the introduction of creatures themselves into what we
can allude to as the ebb and flow of the divine life itself.[19]

It can therefore be said that Eckhart, at least through this
last characteristic, has managed all the same, with a stock
of Neoplatonic ideas, reworked with unheard-of boldness,
to express what, in Christianity, according to Marius Vic-
torinus himself, the Latin translator of Plotinus, transports
the most decidedly the Christian God well beyond the god
of Neoplatonists, which remains the most beautiful of the
lifeless gods of Greece: in the unique transcendence and immanence of the one God who is "the Living One who gives
life".[20]

Speculative Developments
and Spiritual Enlightenments

One would be right to judge that the preceding developments, highly characteristic of Eckhart as a thinker, constitute spiritually ambiguous attainments. Are they not swollen
with equivocations, revealed as much in an immediate lack
of comprehension as in persistent misunderstandings? If this
Neoplatonism will never lose a certain sympathy among
Christians because of the vigor with which it pursued an
intellectual orientation in search of the spiritual, neither will
it ever cease to favor confusion that is injurious to Christian
authenticity.[21]

[19] Cf. what McGinn sums up in his study cited above in note 10.
[20] Cf. Mary T. Clark, "A Neoplatonic Commentary on the Christian
Trinity", 24 ff. of the volume *Neoplatonism and Christian Thought*, see above,
note 16.
[21] See the essay devoted to "The Problem of the Reality and Multiplicity
of Divine Ideas in Christian Neoplatonism", by Norris Clarke, 109 ff., still
in the same volume.

Without always avoiding this danger, Eckhart offers some speculative developments of the Hadewigian tradition that, by bringing it invaluable clarifications, remain incontestable spiritual attainments. Such, in the first place, is his concept of the "ground" of the soul (*Grund*),[22] which certainly helps to concretize what we call the exemplarism of Hadewijch. One might note that the latter, at least once, seems to have anticipated this development when she tells us that the more one descends to the ground of one's soul, the more one draws near what could be called the ground of God,[23] which is very Augustinian.

In Eckhart, however, if this notion of the *Grund* becomes a fundamental piece of spirituality, the manner in which he expresses himself in its regard is not without creating again a suspicion of pantheism. For he himself declares to us straight out that the ground of the soul and this ground of God are one and the same thing, which itself seems to be difficult to distinguish from the Deity, in the sense in which he understands it. It is thus that he does not hesitate to drop the statement, without further explanation, that there is something in the soul—evidently that ground to which he again gives the name "spark"[24]—that is properly uncreated.[25] Yet, once again, it is necessary to discern what he understands by this, in a form that is, up to this point, paradoxical. And that, of course, is itself revealed to be very rich not only with perception of mystical experience but with positive spiritual implications.

---

[22] See on this point the introduction of Jeanne Ancelet-Hustache in the first volume of the *Sermons*, 26ff.

[23] See Letter 18 of Hadewijch, 85ff. in the Hart edition, as well as the translator's note in the Porion edition, 147.

[24] Cf. the introductions of Jeanne Ancelet-Hustache, *Sermons*.

[25] Ibid.

The ground of the soul, in fact, such as Eckhart understands it, is quite simply what we are, not actually in ourselves, but really in the eternal view that God carries of us.
As this view implies, with our creation, our supernatural vocation to a share, wholly gratuitous, of course, in the divine
life itself, he can say that this ground belongs to us from all
eternity, insofar as God never planned to create us indepen-
dently of this vocation to share his life. And if one rightly
observes that, through the Fall, we have lost the grace that
elevated us to this supernatural existence, it is essential to
God's plan that it be returned to us through the redemptive
Incarnation of the Son of God in our flesh. In that sense,
it is very true that there is something uncreated in us: our
vocation, in the view of God himself, inseparable from our
creation. One might say that this is, fundamentally, like the
very root of our existence, while it is also its ultimate end.

After that, it does not take much explanation to understand what Eckhart means when he describes the soul as
being a mirror destined to reflect the Divinity in what is
most essential to it and made with that very thing in view.[26]

The union without mode or intermediary[27] that he proposes as the final end of the created soul is likewise this
association, for which we have been made, to the trinitarian
life: making us son in the Son, and carried with him in his
return of love to this Father in whom the divine Essence is
directly revealed as being the Love that is nothing but pure
generosity, gift, not only of all that one has but of all that
one is.

In close relation to this last point, we find, in Eckhart,
two lines of development that are, actually, simply an explanation of what constitutes perhaps the most realistic, and

[26] Ibid.
[27] See the same commentary, 34ff.

at the same time purely spiritual, element of Hadewijch's spirituality.

One is his insistence on what he describes in one sermon as "the noble man" (an adjective, let us recall, particularly dear to Hadewijch).[28] What this expression covers is precisely the realism of our filiation, which is undoubtedly adoptive but, in our insertion in the Son, a reciprocal effect of his Incarnation in our own flesh and, as Saint John himself says: not at all, therefore, a legal fiction but a mysterious reality. This is obviously what Eckhart wants to express when he says that we have been effectively engendered by the Father, just like the Unique One, from whom we have become inseparable by his birth in us.

The other line is his insistence on poverty,[29] going to the point of a complete emptiness with respect to all that is not the nakedness that is itself proper to the divine Essence: nothing, in short, but being empty of self, stripped of everything insofar as living only in the other, the Father living in the Son, and the Son in the Father, through the proper Spirit of the Father who rests on him as the very Spirit of his filiation.

Here we must insert a development particularly dear to Eckhart, it seems, and of which we must say that, if it is very speculative in principle, it is nonetheless spiritually enlightening. And this is his exposition on the interrelationship between what he calls the *Abegescheidenheit* and the *Gelazenheit*.[30] The first, the *Abegescheidenheit*, is detachment, the ascetical renunciation to any attachment to whatever might

---

[28] *Sermon* 15, 138.

[29] Cf. *Sermon* 52, same translation, vol. 2, 138ff.

[30] On this complex relationship, see the texts cited in the index to Reiner Schürmann, *Maître Eckhart ou la joie errante* (Paris: Denoël, 1972). See also the introductions of J. Ancelet-Hustache to *Sermons* 52 and 53 of vol. 2, as well as 62, 68 and especially 79 of vol. 3.

be limited. This detachment frees us to abandon ourselves
to the supreme grace, an abandonment that is the *Gelazen-*
heit that carries us into this unfathomable disinterestedness,
this personal life in the loss of self in the other, which is so
characteristic of the Deity itself. Yet, if the *Abegescheidenheit*
is the ascetical condition without which our delivery to divine love would remain illusory, in depth it is itself the effect of the *Gelazenheit.* Our detachment, in fact, is sustained,
fostered, by this taking possession of our being, invaded by
grace. We find here once again the attraction, the engulfing,
of which Hadewijch spoke, in the ebb and flow of divine
Love.

Finally, as we have already said, this birth in us of Christ,
of which Eckhart speaks, in this respect more in line with
the Fathers than with Hadewijch, is obviously one with the
full accomplishment of our incorporation to the Son, born
of our flesh, which makes us, as we have seen, son of his own
communicated filiation.

Ruusbroec: Heir and Illuminator
of the Hadewigian Tradition

Whatever may be Eckhart's both mixed and dazzling merits,
the one who contributed more and better than anyone in
transmitting and illuminating the entire content as well as
the exact meaning of the Hadewigian tradition was neither
Eckhart nor any of his most honorable disciples, like Tauler
or Suso, whatever their respective gifts might be. To discover him, we must return from the banks of the Rhine to
the Flemish country: no longer the rich Antwerp milieu,
rich in culture and faith as well as in more commonplace
goods, but that Brussels region, which, in the fourteenth

century, was still far from having the economic, political
or cultural preponderance of the old harbor city. It is, in
fact, in the most humble Dutch dialect (thiois) that Ruusbroec, devoid, for his part, of the aristocratic distinction of
his predecessor, was nevertheless to convey and effectively
prolong her heritage, during centuries when she herself remained practically unknown.[31]

Jean Gerson, whose own spiritual heritage, although immensely influential, enclosed as it is in a wholly modern
psychologism, is very modest in its assets, was to criticize
him with a wholly professorial pedantry, believing him to be
the victim of an erroneous metaphysics. In fact, Ruusbroec
himself did not have intellectual aims, but his theological
thought, as little pretentious as it is, is more flexible than
that of this Parisian schoolmaster. As for his spirituality, it is
one of the greatest contemplative ones known to the Christian tradition. One could scarcely say as much of the pedant
who was at least deluding himself a bit about his capacity
to catch him out.[32]

At an early age, Ruusbroec was taken out of his native
village by an uncle, a Canon of Saint Gudule, Jan Hinck-
aert, undoubtedly struck by his gifts, and the name of Ruusbroec, which attached itself to him, simply recalls this ru-
ral origin. Born in 1293, he was already a priest in 1317,
first vicar then chaplain of the collegiate church. It was thus
close to this uncle that the nephew must have begun a very
lively ministry centered on spiritual formation. We are told
that he avoided going to town as much as possible, while

---

[31] On Ruusbroec, see, in the special issue of *Vie spirituelle* (November 1982)
the article by Johan Bonny, "Ian van Ruusbroec" (pp. 666ff.), which includes
an up-to-date bibliography.

[32] See A. Combes, *Essai sur la critique de Ruysbroeck par Gerson*, 4 vols. (Paris:
Vrin, 1945–1972).

he gave his attention to cautioning his directees against doctrinal errors, or at least against the pseudo-mystical follies of a more or less amorphous but at that time singularly influential movement: the "Brothers of the Free Spirit". We learn in particular that he was worried about the influence exercised in Brussels by a woman named Bloemardine. Let us note that one scholar has been found (we always have, in this field, too, people inclined to the strangest suppositions) to think, not only despite the dates but without a shadow of probability, that this name designated . . . Hadewijch herself!

It is evident, moreover, that, when Ruusbroec took Holy Orders, the deviations that were already causing alarm in the Rhineland at the time of Eckhart had only grown and been embellished, and certainly no less in the Netherlands than in the diocese of Cologne and its surroundings. One famous treatise, seeking to claim Meister Eckhart's doctrine as its authority, which puts a Sister Catherine on stage giving advice to her director, is perhaps all the more instructive as no moral laxity is declared in it but only an indifference to all forms of traditional worship as well as of ascetical life.[33] The good sister, who easily declares: "Father, rejoice: from now on, I am God!" and who has promptly dropped all belief in hell as well as in paradise, judging the Resurrection to be superfluous, is only a pious crazy who takes herself to be a saint. Examples of this kind have never been wanting in the Church, but, in this period, they abounded!

It was first of all in order to preserve the most pious faithful from it that Ruusbroec in Brussels wrote his first trea-

---

[33] *Meister Eckhart: Essential Sermons, Commentaries, Treatises and Defense*, trans. B. McGinn, see note 6 above.

tise: The *Kingdom of Lovers*.[34] No sooner than it existed in manuscript than copies were to be found everywhere. But, far from being satisfied with it, he judged it insufficient: neither clear nor precise enough. He therefore set to work without further delay, and this time the result would be the *Spiritual Espousals*, his masterpiece. In order to respond to questions raised by reading it, he would take up his pen once again, and this would be the case on many occasions up until his final years.

But, in 1343, he decided to retire, with a few friends, to a tranquil place, a slight distance away, whose name alone gives sufficient description: Groenendael, the Green Valley. In the beginning, no one envisaged a monastic or religious foundation. But, at the end of a short time, they let themselves be persuaded to affiliate themselves with the Canons Regular, and Ruusbroec became the prior of the little community. Henceforth, immersing himself more and more in prayer and reflection, he scarcely ever left this retreat, although he did receive there a flood of visitors.

His first biographer, Pomerius, cites in particular a certain doctor in theology, a Dominican, whom the manuscripts call Canclaer, but who might very well have been Tauler (the writing of that time lent itself to such a deformation).[35] Even if this correction is nothing but a reverie of overly imaginative historians, Ruusbroec certainly knew Eckhart, although he never quotes him; in any case, the pious community cook, John Leeuwen, must have been acquainted, if not with the work of the Meister, then at least with what

---

[34] Dom James Wiseman provided an excellent English translation of the principal texts (New York, 1987), and preceded it with a remarkable introduction.

[35] Cf. J. Wiseman, 25.

some adventurous disciples, more or less deranged in the
same way as the famous Catherine, drew from it, for the
worthy cook, between two services, had concocted a rather
spicy refutation of these horrors.[36]

There is no doubt, for example, that the prior himself, as
well as this confrère who quotes Hadewijch by name, had
in hand a manuscript of her work, and that she had over
him as well as his successor an influence that is difficult to
measure but undeniable.

His literary activity at Groenendael was no less fruitful
than in Brussels. Once again, however, it may be judged that
he had given the best of himself in the *Spiritual Espousals*,
with a few refinements and complements brought to it by
later treatises.

He died on December 2, 1381, and, despite the quibbling of Gerson, he would soon be considered one of the
blessed. Yet it was not until 1909 that he was officially beatified; Tauler also, who died in 1361, had been beatified
only in 1832, and Suso, who died in 1366, one year before
the latter.

What place shall we assign to Ruusbroec, what importance should we recognize in him, especially in the perspective that remains ours here, in the development of this mystical flowering at the origin of which Hadewijch seems to
have had an unrivalled role?

Johan Bonny,[37] his fellow countryman to whom we owe
one of the better recent studies, goes into ecstasy over the
qualities as thinker and writer that he recognizes in Ruusbroec. Since our knowledge of the Flemish language, in its

---

[36] See the article on him by Bernard Spaapen in the *Dictionnaire de spiritualité*.
[37] Bonny, "Ian van Ruusbroec" in *Vie spirituelle* (November 1982) 668.

different historical varieties, is more rudimentary, we will refrain from picking a quarrel with him on this point. But we must admit that the distinctions and enumerations to which Ruusbroec attaches great value seem to us, rather, to be dependent on one of the most lamentable contrivances cultivated by medieval ratiocinators, and his laboriously wrought imagery some of the most annoying examples of bad taste that this period has given us. On the other hand, his spiritual teaching makes it easy to forget all these overly elaborate decorations, and the personality, which, despite these weaknesses, still shows through better from his writings than from the admiring reports of his contemporaries, assuredly deserves our warm sympathy.

If, then, we try to define the personal contribution of Ruusbroec to what we have called the Hadewigian tradition, the first point, and not the least, results from the pastoral concerns brought out above, which pressured the young priest into taking up his pen so soon.

His entire testimony, in fact, is framed by a twofold and very strict distinction: between authentic Christian life and contemplation, on the one hand, and the whole tendency toward pantheism as well as quietism. This is all the more remarkable, on his part, since he is in no way inferior to Meister Eckhart when it is a question of affirming a mysticism for which the Fathers of the Greek Church had already formed the concepts of "divinization", indeed, of "deification".[38]

The beginning of the *Spiritual Espousals* is concerned with a whole new personal expression of another theme coming

[38] On the meaning to be given these words, see our *Mysterion* (Paris: OEIL, 1986), 281ff.

from patristics: that of the three ways, or three phases of development, of the spiritual life. He, for his part, calls these the active life, the interior life and the contemplative life, to which should be added what he will call, in a little later treatise, *La Pierre étincelante*, the "common life".

The active life, of course, is that of the virtues and cultural and ethical as well as ascetical practices. But one point of capital importance is that, if it is necessary to begin with this, it is not a question of seeing it as a mere prelude to what will follow. On the contrary, it is essential to the authenticity of the interior life, and equally to the contemplative life, that the attainments of the active life be pursued and perfected. We must say the same, in this regard, of what he understands by the "common life".[39]

This is not at all some kind of "social" life, as we would say today. It is the contemplative life itself that makes it possible and that demands it. Just as this contemplative life, in fact, for the Christian, does not do away with our relations with the Persons of the Trinity—quite the contrary, in attaining the divine reality even in its living unity, it hurries us, so to speak, into a real participation in those inexpressible relations themselves that constitute the Three Persons—this life, therefore, could not make our relations with our brothers indifferent but, rather, transfigures them. This, undoubtedly, corresponds to what Eckhart told us of the close relation in God himself between the *bullitio* of the Divine Persons and the *ebullitio* that extends, so to speak, the life of the Trinity into that of creation. But it is very typical of Ruusbroec that, instead of expressing himself in a metaphysical way, he does it in terms of a spirituality that

---

[39] Cf. Bonny, 688ff.

remains wholly practical even though it springs from the contemplation of the most elevated objects of faith.

Actually, his entire concept of communal life corresponding to the highest summits of spiritual ascension springs from the development he gives to the theme, coming from Hadewijch, of the ebb and flow of the trinitarian life.

For Ruusbroec, effectively, just as in God, God the Father, Son and Holy Spirit, the activity, the eternal fecundity of the divine life producing the diversity of Persons coincides with the repose in which the Father, the origin of all, also "engulfs" the Son, on whom the Spirit of the Father reposes, the Spirit of filiation, likewise, in the soul that has arrived at the height of his progress in God, the repose of contemplation, here below, should be pursued in an activity of fraternal charity of a depth unimaginable up to then. Otherwise, we could not henceforth be united with that ebb and flow that are equally essential to the living unity of the trinitarian life. That, properly speaking, is the supreme participation of the believer in the divine *agapē*.

Another development of great importance contributed by Ruusbroec to the testimony of Hadewijch appears even as early as the second book of the *Spiritual Espousals*. It is the way in which he clarifies those proofs of love that are so necessary to its development in us. In order to understand it, we must observe a threefold distinction that Ruusbroec makes between three levels of our conscience: there is, first of all, affectivity, which is for him linked to the body, to its insertion into the physical world, and which is what he calls the "heart". Then come the three inseparable faculties of memory, understanding and will. Finally, there is the profound unity of the human spirit. God comes to us in Christ first of all through affectivity, by obtaining

increasingly elevated sensible consolations for us. But the
latter are transcended through a trial of sensible desolation
that serves to prepare us for a simplification of the memory, retaining only the "one thing necessary", while the understanding of the mystery of faith is illuminated, and the
will is inflamed by a love that transcends the sensible. The
transition from the merely interior life to the contemplative
life will be set in motion by a directly divine "touch" (the
beginning of unmediated union).

Received passively through this "unity of spirit" that transcends its distinct faculties, the above-mentioned "touch"
creates in the soul an agonizing need for God. It is what
he calls the "tempest", or again, the "battle of Love". He
himself explains what he means by that:

> In this very deep encounter, this very intimate and ardent
> approach, each spirit (ours and that of God himself) is
> wounded by love. They cast onto each other a dazzling
> light and their faces are thus mutually revealed. As a result,
> the two try to outdo each other in love. Each asks for what
> the other is and, in turn, offers him what he himself is. As
> a result, they lose themselves in each other.[40]

The very word "touch", in Flemish *gherinen*, as Helmut
Hatzfeld was the first to suggest,[41] may very well have been
chosen by Ruusbroec in order to prepare us to enter, in what
follows, into the divine "flow" of the intratrinitarian life:
in Flemish, *rinen* is in fact the verb for "to flow out".

In fact, what has just been described will be given by
Ruusbroec himself as "the most interior exercise that a per-

---

[40] *L'Ornement des noces spirituelles*, II, 2/3 C.
[41] Cf. Helmut Hatzfeld, "The Influence of Ramon Lull and Ian van Ruysbroeck on the Language of the Spanish Mystics", in *Traditio*, vol. 4 (1946),
383ff.

son illuminated by a created light [obviously that of sancti-
fying grace, according to Saint Thomas] can practice."

As he will again say:

> That is the final intermediary between God and his crea-
> ture. Above this "touch", in the being [now] in repose of
> spirit, floats an incomprehensible splendor: that of the sub-
> lime Trinity from which this "touch" proceeds. Then God
> lives and reigns in the spirit [of the man], and this spirit in
> God.[42]

The properly contemplative life will be to be taken and
carried along in this "flow".

The third book of the *Spiritual Espousals* is devoted to it.
But, before coming to it, we must at least observe that the
two "nights", of the senses and then of the spirit, that we
will find described by Saint John of the Cross have very close
antecedents in the two crises, the two passages, solicited by
grace, first from the "heart" to the "spirit", then from the
"spirit" of the man directly "touched" by the divine Spirit
to his blessed fall into the "flow" of the very life of God,
into the living Unity of his Trinity.[43]

This finally introduces us, as far as possible, to what is
evidently inexpressible even as Ruusbroec gives us his own
understanding of divine exemplarism, which is, for him as
for Hadewijch, the eternal foundation of our supernatural
vocation.

For him:

> Through the eternal birth [of the Son], all creatures have
> proceeded eternally, before their creation in time. God has
> thus seen and known them in himself, as distinct in his

[42] A continuation of the same text quoted above (with reference given in
note 40).

[43] See below, 120.

living ideas and distinct from himself, although not different in all respects, for all that is in God is God. . . . In this
divine image, all creatures thus have an eternal life apart
from themselves, as in their eternal Exemplar.[44]

He will consequently say that:

It is in this eternal image and resemblance that the Holy
Trinity has created us. God, consequently, wants for us to
go out of ourselves in order to enter into this divine light,
pursuing supernaturally this image that is our own life and
for us to possess it with him, actively and blessedly in a state
of eternal beatitude.[45]

When we have reached that stage, he will further say,

We become capable of contemplating God with God without an intermediary, in the divine light [the splendor of
which we receive emanating from the Son], in such a way
that the contemplative is transformed and becomes one
with this light by which he sees and that he sees, and he
is made "one single spirit with the Spirit of God".[46]

The conclusion of the book, and, we might say, of all
Ruusbroec's teaching, will thus be:

May we blissfully possess the essential Unity and clearly
contemplate the Unity in the Trinity, may the divine love
grant it to us, for it never sends a beggar away.[47]

In other words, this union with, this assimilation to God
is only pure grace, but it is the grace that God intends to
grant us in eternity. The contemplative can hope to antici-
pate it in a way, he again stresses, that remains "dark", but

[44] *Ornement*, III, 3A.
[45] Ibid., III, 3B.
[46] Ibid., III, 4.
[47] The final words of this book III.

with that darkness, as Pseudo-Dionysius recalls, which in the end is but one with the "inaccessible light where God resides" and where alone his love can, or rather, wishes, if we consent, to lead us.[48]

From Tauler
to Angelus Silesius

Tauler and Suso, especially the former, certainly had a considerable role in the spread of the mystical tradition that is the subject of our study. In particular, in relation to that other popular movement that would be called the "Friends of God" (which has been insufficiently studied), they contributed, in opposition to the heterodox tendencies of the Brothers of the Free Spirit, to the spreading of this spirituality well beyond conventual circles: both among the laity as well as among secular priests.

Tauler, first of all, through his sermons, both in monasteries and in cathedral or parish churches, proved to be, in this regard, a genius at popularizing. Over and above his insistence, not only particularly rigorous but very concrete, on the inseparability of mysticism and a reform of all existence even in its most profane aspects, his originality is notable in a certain rectification of vocabulary. He does employ the Eckhartian *Grunt*, but he is careful to stress its transcendence in relation to our immediate experience, for example, by insisting that it is actually a question of an *Abgrunt*: of a beyond ourselves, whose place is only in the abyss of the divine thought concerning us. Or, better still, he will substitute the *Germuet*, which recalls a theme dear to Maximus the Confessor: of our divinization through a "disposition"

[48] Cf. the fifth *Letter* of Dionysius and I Timothy 6:16.

created in us with regard to the divine Essence but which does not transmute ours for all that.

Let us recall again the Marian sense that he, like Hade-wijch, gives to the theme of the birth of Christ in us, a theme that was patristic before being Eckhartian.

Although he often, and for rather long periods, left his native Strasbourg, his death in the monastery of Saint Nicholas of Ondes, on the other side of Ill, near his sister, who was a Dominican nun, and his tomb, the sole surviving relic, in the hideously Wilhelminian Neue Kirche, of the old church of the Preachers that was at its center, symbolize his rootedness in the old Alsacian city.[49]

His local influence can be judged by reading the rather bizarre mystico-apocalyptic and pseudo-historical productions of an admittedly rather banal "Friend of God": the Strasbourg banker Rulman Merswyn, the only known example, before Jaegen in the modern period, of a financier fallen into mysticism.[50]

It is more embarrassing to evaluate Suso.[51] This other Dominican, this time from the region of Constance, is a figure whose romanticism enchanted even as serious a historian of our mystics as Madame Ancelet-Hustache. She herself, however, was forced to recognize the outrageously fantastic character of the alleged autobiography that has long been attributed to him. But it must be admitted that

[49] The best recent study on Tauler is that of Josef Schmidt, in the introduction to *Johannes Tauler: Sermons* (New York: Paulist Press, 1985).

[50] See the study on him by F. Rapp in the *Dictionnaire de spiritualité*. The foundational critical study on the "Friends of God" remains that of Auguste Jundt, published in Paris in 1879.

[51] See, again in *Les Mystiques rhénans*, the article by Jeanne Ancelet-Hustache, "Henri Suso sans fiction", 719ff.

once the stories of terrible and decidedly morbid austerities, which have been largely responsible for his fame, are dissipated, there remains of him a personality that is undoubtedly sympathetic but that does not contribute much to the Eckhartian tradition beyond inconsistent fantasies and a sensitivity that is more touching than well placed in this context.

More worthy of attention is *Theologia germanica*, the work of a secular priest.[52] It long enchanted Luther[53] and is at least a witness to the healthy popularity that Rheno-Flemish mysticism managed to win in both clerical and lay circles. But, without any doubt, what was to assure its influence in all of Europe, and well after the end of the Middle Ages, was the Latin translation of the *Mirror* owed to the Batavian Franciscan Henri Herp (better known as Harphius), which is scarcely more than a popularization of Ruusbroec, and especially the compilations in the same scholarly language of all our authors (except of course for Hadewijch herself) that are owed to Surius, a Carthusian of Cologne.[54]

One might consider the last local scion of Germanic mysticism to be found in the paradoxical couplets of a Lutheran who converted to Franciscanism: Johannes Scheffler, alias Angelus Silesius.[55] A few excerpts from his *Cherubic Pilgrim* can provide the best conclusion to the present chapter.

[52] One thinks of a chaplain for the Teutonic Knights.

[53] See the excellent study by Bengt R. Hoffman, *Luther and the Mystics: A Re-examination of Luther's Spiritual Experience and His Relationship to the Mystics* (Minneapolis: Augsburg Pub., 1976).

[54] See on these two popularizers the article in the *Dictionnaire de spiritualité* on "Harphius (Herp)", by E. Gullick and O. de Vegel, and that in the *Dictionnaire de théologie catholique* on "Surius", by S. Autore.

[55] On Angelus Silesius, see the introduction by H. Plard to his edition and translation of the *Pélerin cherubinique* (Paris, 1946).

The creature is truly in God.
The creature is more in God than in itself:
May it die and remain in him forever!

There we have exemplarism.

Mystical marriage:
What joy it must be when God espouses his fiancée
In his eternal Word, through his Spirit!

And here are the "Spiritual Espousals".

God-man:
Think, then! God is changed into me, attains my misery
So that I might attain the Kingdom and be able to change
    into Him!

Our "divinization" as fruit of his Incarnation.

Spiritual birth:
May the Spirit of God touch you with his essence,
and the Child of eternity be born in you.

The birth of Christ in us.

The spiritual Mary:
I must be Mary and God must be born in me
So that he may grant me beatitude in his eternity.

The same thing, but according to Tauler just as according
to Hadewijch.
And again:

The more abandoned one is, but more divine:
The saints are so inebriated with the Deity of God
That they are lost, engulfed in him!

And, to conclude:

Why does God have repose and joy?
Because God is three in One, He has repose and joy:
Repose comes from the Unity, Joy from the bosom of
the Trinity![56]

---

[56] The couplets quoted are numbers 193 and 183 of the first book, 20 of
the third book, 103 of the second book, 23 of the first book, 210 of the first
book and 283 of the fifth book.

III

TERESA OF AVILA

From the Mystics of the North
to the Mystics of Spain

During the sixteenth century in Spain, we witness a spiritual revival whose blossoming bears a striking similarity to that for which we have given examples from the Flemish and Rhenish lands in the thirteenth and fourteenth centuries. Here again, the initiative first comes from a woman, but the major developments, this time, come, not from a masculine pleiad, but from a man who was, moreover, not simply a reader or merely an indirect heir of the woman who is the point of departure for it all, but her main collaborator, whatever role others may have played in these new developments.

Yet again, it was a woman, at the origin of everything, who took the lead in this remarkable renewal of spiritual experience, while it was a man, John of the Cross, who both tried to justify speculatively the experience of Teresa of Avila, into which he had entered after her and, in doing so, brought into focus, by clarifying it critically, the directly spiritual testimony that she expressed. But it is, once again, to her that we owe the initiative for this resurgence.

What adds to the interest of this new cooperation between a woman, at the point of departure, and a man, in her footsteps, is not only that they actually collaborated but that they are both incontestable saints and exceptional spirits, both of whom the Church has recognized, not just by canonization, but with the title of Doctor.

On the other hand, there can be no doubt that, for her as well as for him, their experiences and what they drew from them are indebted, more or less directly, to the Rheno-Flemish heritage. Their vocation, like the way in which they were to develop its possibilities, bear the mark of their predecessors, however personal what they themselves added may remain.

As for Teresa of Avila, it is very clear that she received encouragement and direction through two popularizers and adapters of this Northern heritage: the Franciscans Francisco de Osuna and Bernardino de Laredo:[1] the *Abecedarios* of the former and *La Subida del Monte Sion* of the latter. It is also more than probable that John of the Cross, who was equally familiar with them, had in addition some first-hand contact with some Rheno-Flemish texts themselves, either by Harphius or, particularly, by Surius, in Latin, but probably also in Spanish translations, which were already circulating.

Yet, as Jean Orcibal is the first to insist,[2] and it is he who provides the best inventory of contacts and borrowings, this in no way signifies that the experiences of the two Castilians are not entirely personal or even that their in-depth reflections on the latter lose any of their originality to the degree that they knew and used the heritage of the Northern mystics.

Rather, what we have here is a remarkable case of a tradi-

---

[1] The *Third Spiritual Alphabet* by Osuna would be read by Teresa at her uncle's home, and the treatise by Laredo would play a major role in reassuring her about her extraordinary experiences.

[2] Jean Orcibal, *Saint Jean de la Croix et les mystiques rhéno-flamands* (Paris, 1966).

tion as faithfully received as renewed, vivified and developed in the most creative way through no less authentic experiences as well as through new reflections of rare richness.

The milieu in which they wrote, moreover, presents both striking analogies with and radical differences from the Northern milieu. And, here again, there is undoubtedly a certain continuity, though with entirely local variations. In particular, Teresa and John, who have become eminently influential and respected masters for modern Christians, had, like their predecessors, to react against ideas and to distinguish themselves in a milieu characterized by a mysticism that was not only anarchical but extremely mixed. There were no longer "Brothers of the Free Spirit", but rather *alumbrados*: the "illuminated", who singularly resembled them and who, themselves, were not without some more or less direct relationship with the earlier movement, although they offered some features *sui generis*.[3]

To take just one detail, which applies to all the other Castilians, orthodox or heterodox, but particularly to John of the Cross, the opposition of light to shadows or, more precisely, of night to day, is found in Spain as in the North. But many commentators miss the fact that the same image in the plains of Flanders and the valley of the Rhine can assume different meanings in Castile. In a country where light is rare and obscurity all too usual, the night seems to be pure negativity, while the farther south one moves, on the Iberian peninsula, the more it is broad daylight that seems intolerable and night to be the time when one feels revived. Thus John of the Cross' "nights", in particular, have often been too simply interpreted. As we shall see, to plunge

[3] The fundamental study of this movement remains that of Marcelino Menéndez y Pelayo, *Historia de los heterodoxos españoles*, 7 vols. (Madrid, 1911–1932).

into the night is not only a trial: it is in the fullness of the night, and not beyond, that the most positive experience will come.[4]

That being said, and although Teresa of Avila is more familiar to us, through her letters, her *Life* and the account of her *Foundations*, than Hadewijch, who, despite her all-too-fascinating literary legacy, remains a mystery to us, there are many analogies between the personality of the Antwerp mystic and that of the Castilian, not without, of course, some differences that are just as marked.[5]

With Hadewijch, aristocratic delicacy, entrancing poetry, enhanced no doubt by the ignorance in which we remain about her precise identity, contrast with the popular good sense and readily earthly realism of Teresa. That does not prevent them both from having been and remaining always strongly influenced by the same style of chivalric novels, which continued from one century to the other.

But, with Hadewijch, we find these novels joined to a period of quintessential refinement, while, with Teresa, we are already very close to Don Quixote, when not to Sancho Panza: in other words, the decidedly unrealistic fantasy and jovial realism that are blended in Teresa clash with the wild idealism of Hadewijch, without ever, for all that, being so very far away from each other.

The major difference, however, despite the most marked similarities, is in the immediate religious context of each.

[4] My attention was drawn to this point by Father Juan-Miguel Garrigues.

[5] On Saint Teresa, the best work in French, even though written for the general public, is her biography by Marcelle Auclair, which has been translated into English by Kathleen Pond (Petersham, Mass.: St. Bede's, 1988). The critical edition of her works is that of Father Silverio de S. Teresa, 2d ed. (Burgos, 1930). The most authoritative English translation of her collected works has been published by the Institute of Carmelite Studies in Washington, D.C.

That of Hadewijch was the expectation of a reform that is
passionately desired but already not without equivocation.
For Teresa, it was a reform gone astray, having already provoked a response that was principally but not exclusively
negative. She was caught between two fires, and for her the
temptation might have been, no longer that of indistinct
enthusiasm, but that of discouragement, though of course
she would in the end give in to one no more than to the
other.

But it is necessary to measure the overall gravity of the
situation in which Teresa was going to find herself by this
fact. Hadewijch was also in possession of a carefully worked
out education that put her to reading not only contemporary
French books of chivalry but all Latin Christian literature.

Teresa, for her part, would have only little and generally
rather mediocre Castilian books of piety (except for the two
works already cited, which are only fair popularizations), after having been crammed, like all girls of her generation,
with the most staggering but also the most decadent productions of the chivalric age. Hadewijch was nourished on
a liturgy she understood without difficulty. Teresa would
recite all her life as a Carmelite an office that was nearly
incomprehensible to her and, for want of accessible translations, would never have anything but a vague idea even of
the prayers of the Mass, which she attended more than she
participated in, like all her contemporaries, both male and
female, with very few exceptions.

As for the Bible, let us not speak of it: except for a few
sentences or paraphrases of the Gospels in translation, a few
biblical narratives received second hand, it was from then
on, for a woman or a layman without an exceptional education, strictly forbidden territory. Her first posthumous
editor, Luis de Leon, priest and university man that he was,

had to spend years in the jails of the Inquisition for having disregarded this.

That, under these conditions, Teresa was able to produce a work with a balance, with a spiritual fullness such as hers seems extraordinary.

The Career of Teresa of Avila

Before approaching this work, let us recall at least briefly the whole of her advance toward God. It is not an exaggeration to say that one can discern in it how providence led her to super-eminent sanctity but through a series of circumstances that would seem to tend directly toward a morbid exaltation mixed with a piety that was made wholly of sentiment, not to say sentimentality.

Despite what we have already pointed out in her quite undeniably "common" character, she belonged, if not to the aristocracy, in any case to the most honorable upper class— something we cannot know with any certainty about Hadewijch, as great a lady as she was! But it must be recalled that in the southern Latin nations, and very especially Spain, there is even today no distinct separation between the highest nobility and what one would elsewhere call the rabble. To tell the truth, in Spain, there could be, as everywhere else and in all circles, scroungers and swindlers, but rabble did not exist. The least of the beggars might rightly consider himself a *hidalgo* and, to be great in Spain, one is no less perfectly at ease with the working classes, putting them at ease, if need be, with one's first words.

In fact, Teresa de Ahumada y Cepeda, born in that Avila amid the mountains that can look as if it were always set in a Middle Ages of chivalric novels, had very early and always retained, along with the oversensitive pride of the Castilian nobility, the good nature that is easily more than pleasant and, above all, the fearlessness, the amazing activity of a race that, although living in climactic conditions that are paralyzing for everyone else, seems incapable of knowing rest or quite simply of staying put. Her adventures as a child, with a brother who must have been delighted to find in her this would-be boy, not perhaps without grumbling at times at being bothered by this kid who could probably be as despotic as irrepressible, were naturally marked by the twofold stamp of an exalted religion and of a chivalric fantasy already turned quixotic. Fortunately there was an uncle to lead these monkeys en route to a dream of martyrdom back to their father's house! After that, it is not without interest that this same uncle apparently was to supply a somewhat more mature Teresa with her first pious reading of quality.

All the same, this mischievous, motherless girl,[6] who was not only adventurous but fairly restless, with a phenomenal intelligence but an intemperate imagination, was soon and for a rather long time to give dangerous signs of a tendency toward hysteria, if not of a total mental and physiological derangement. After the education, apparently as poor in matters of real culture as in solid piety, received in one of the convents that could pass for being relatively serious in the general laxity of men and women religious of that time, it is difficult to estimate the part of deep faith and that of superficial romanticism in the motives that made her enter a still more degenerated Carmel. She had to pass through twenty years, crossed by crises in which neurosis is evident, in

---

[6] Teresa's mother, the second wife of her father, had died when Teresa was only thirteen years old.

order finally to encounter a genuine vocation in her search
for God and to surrender herself to it from then on without
slackening.

What is astonishing, even transfixing, is that after all that
went before, with so deficient an education, with an entrance into a still worse religious life and, above all, with
a temperament that was at the least clearly unbalanced, she
was able suddenly to set off so straight and to persevere in
so sure a line toward personal holiness, as well as toward
what must well be called the most extraordinary missionary activity (although entirely enclosed, or nearly so, in a
multitude of cloistered foundations, first of women, then
of men as well).

Teresa de Ahumada without any doubt is the product of
exceptional grace, but the path had been prepared by giving
her, along with a trembling sensitivity that at the beginning
and for a long time was not the healthiest, a keenness of understanding and judgment and a strength of will that were
equally uncommon.

A few chronological indications will suffice to give an idea
of the personal development and work that this woman of
precarious health, the victim of a nervous system balanced
only with difficulty, succeeded in achieving, first on home
ground, then in books that are but a series of brilliant im-
provisations, cast onto paper in the midst of perpetual ag-
itation, combined in an almost incredible way with an elevated interior life and, finally, a purity that have scarcely
been paralleled.

Born on March 28, 1515 (the year, thus, that Luther began to make himself known), provided with seven brothers
and four sisters, educated (more or less well) by the Augus-
tinians of Our Lady of Grace, after some time spent in a
worldliness that was apparently innocent but excited by the

reading of the most frenzied novels of chivalry, she was led to the Carmel of the Incarnation at Avila through the reading of some edifying old books of her uncle (fortunately, on the whole, rather well chosen), more through the fear of hell than by the love of God, on November 2, 1536. One year later, she was received there for Profession.

At first profoundly happy with her decision, she nevertheless spent, in this monastery, twenty years of a superficial religious life that were not, properly speaking, scandalous but, like more or less all others of her time, very lax. After that, a weakening, indeed, a collapse of her health seemed to demand her exclaustration, and she went to Becedas, to family property, where she was attacked by all kinds of troubles: persistent fever, cardiac weakness, more or less epileptic-type seizures. Finally, she was thought to be consumptive. On the night of August 15, 1539, she was expected to die. Yet, on the following Easter, she seemed sufficiently recovered to return to her monastery.

Yet, already in the autumn of 1538, on a visit to the home of her uncle, she had read the *Third Spiritual Alphabet* by Osuna with interest. We still have her copy, abundantly underlined. What is more, we know that in 1539 she had had a first imaginary vision of Christ, addressing vigorous reproaches to her. Nevertheless, her return to the monastery, which, it seems, was increasingly worldly, signified for her at first only a return to worldliness. In 1543, her father having been seized with a fatal illness, she returned, with him, to the reading of Osuna. But we know that she abandoned this study even before he died, on Christmas Eve.

If we can believe her testimony, from this year until 1555, she abandoned all personal prayer outside the Office recited in choir (of which she, once again, understood very little). In 1555, she had a startling experience of Christ's presence, accompanied by a vision with an inner voice, calling her to fidelity. She read the *Confessions* of Saint Augustine and consulted some Jesuits, recently settled in Avila. Her confessors from this order first had an entirely negative impression of these experiences. She met Saint Francis Borgia (the Duke of Gandia) but, shortly after, lost her Jesuit confessor and seems to have fallen back into frivolous friendships.

One day, reciting the *Veni Creator*, she had a sudden spiritual ecstasy. Two years of uncertainty were still to follow, marked by what she would judge to be diabolical temptations. In 1558, her first intellectual vision (she tells us) of Jesus present at her side, later imaginative visions (again, according to her) of Jesus, either resurrected or on the Cross. After a period of visions accompanied by great devotion to the Rosary, she finally had, in 1559, the famous vision of the cherubim transpiercing her with a dart of fire. In addition, she met Father Balthasar Alvarez, S.J., and took him as confessor. Then she received spiritual advice from the particularly ascetical Franciscan Saint Peter of Alcantara.

As early as 1558, moreover, her pious lay friend, Maria de Ocampo, had suggested that she found a Carmelite reform, returning to the primitive rule that had been more than mitigated in 1432.

Another friend, Doña Guiomar de Ulloa, urged her in the same direction, and Father Balthasar Alvarez approved it in principle.

Her superiors, however, were hesitant, the other sisters at the Incarnation frankly hostile.

In April 1561, her new Jesuit director, Gaspar de Salazar, gave her his entire support. One of her sisters, Doña Juana de Ahumada, bought a house with this in view.

But it was only during her visit to Toledo, at the home of still another friend, Doña Luisa de la Cerda, in April 1562, that she obtained from Rome, assisted by the firm support of Peter of Alcantara, a license in view of the projected foundation. In June, she returned to the monastery of the Incarnation (now under a new Prioress) and finally, on August 24, with the agreement of the Bishop, Don Alvaro de Mendoza, the purchased house was occupied by Teresa and four candidates.

Then followed a period of joy mixed with anxiety about the future. Attacks multiplied, yet she found unexpected support in the person of Bañez, a Dominican theologian from Salamanca. In March 1563, the provincial at last agreed. In April of the same year, the transfer of Teresa and her novices was considered to be a definitive *fait accompli*. The new house became the first reformed monastery, under the name of Saint Joseph, who was dear to Teresa (it was she who served as the source of modern devotion to the foster father of Jesus).

During these last vicissitudes, Teresa had fallen, after Francisco de Osuna, on another Franciscan work, the *Montée du Mont Sion* of Bernardino de Laredo. There she finally found, with a profound relief, a description of her recent experiences. She showed these passages, with an account of her experiences, first to a pious layman, then to a priest; it was then, while on another visit to Toledo, again at the home of Doña Luisa de la Cerda, that she undertook, at the request of her confessor, a written account of her life. Her confessor, then Bañez, having read her first draft, approved it and encouraged her to continue. The whole was completed in 1565.

There was not, at first, any question of publishing this text, but, after she had loaned it to the Princess of Eboli (a fairly foolish pious woman), it began to be circulated and, naturally, attacked. Then Bañez undertook an in-depth reading of it, suggested a few clarifications of detail, and managed, evidently through his insistence and thanks to his personal prestige, to have it sanctioned by the Spanish Inquisition. A first manuscript, from the hand of Saint Teresa herself, and a copy made by her niece Teresita are both today in the Escorial.

We have in this autobiography the basic work in which she gives a fundamental expression of all that will be her teaching, based on an experience clarified by her reading, examined by her first directors, and particularly by the eminent theologian and spiritual master Bañez. It would thus be appropriate to pause here briefly.

The Teaching of the Vida

Teresa's *Life*, already and par excellence, is not only a work in which the exceptional personality of Saint Teresa is ingenuously described but also a literary masterpiece, which can be considered one of the first classics of modern Castilian.

The first ten chapters are a detailed history, both interior and external, of her early years of development up until her contacts with the Jesuits newly arrived in Avila. Then come twelve chapters that are more systematic, but presented as the fruit of her initial experience and which she describes through a comparison with four kinds of water. We will return to this in a moment. Then follow, in chapter twenty-three, several other narrative pages, then, up to the end of chapter twenty-seven, another dissertation on what she calls "locutions". Chapters twenty-eight to thirty-two pick up the history of her interior development again and seem to constitute the end of her first draft. Chapters thirty-three to forty, undoubtedly written later, describe the foundation of Saint Joseph's in Avila. This whole would subsequently be completed by the *Relaciones*, covering the years 1560 to 1581.

It was not until after Teresa's death that the great Salamanca doctor Luis de Leon would edit this work.

This *Life* was to inspire innumerable conversions and religious vocations: the end of the present book will show how one night spent with this volume had that twofold effect on Edith Stein.

It is clear that it is to this *Life* that we must go back in order to find, at its original source, Teresa's spiritual teaching unfolding from her own experience. The chapters noted above, on the theme of the "waters", give us the essence of it. It is advisable, therefore, to follow them with particular attention.

Teresa distinguishes here four different forms, successive in principle, under which the living water of spiritual experience can be received by the soul in search of God.

There is first of all the "well", which is to say, the basic experience that meditation can generate, which she compares to the effort to draw water from wells: let us understand here by this term "meditation" a combination of imagination feeding on gospel scenes, reflection that is like an analysis of its teachings, and finally an act of will striving to draw the vital consequence of it for ourselves.

Here, two points must be emphasized that are often minimized or simply neglected by commentators. The first is that the meditation in question here is an essentially modern type of this kind of exercise, conceived particularly by the contemporaries of Saint Teresa, in a line in which Gerson was one of the first initiators. This line presupposes, first of all, a radical innovation with respect to the whole previous spiritual tradition, notably that of ancient and medieval monasticism. That is to say, instead of suggesting a meditative reading of Scripture, in the school of the liturgy, it is assumed, on the contrary, that Scripture is no longer accessible either to religious or to the laity who do not know Latin, while all biblical translation is now a priori suspect. As for the liturgy, they were already well on the way that would end a little later in seeing it only as "the official form of the external worship of the Church".

All of that resulted, obviously, in a catastrophic combination of the individualism and religious subjectivism of the end of the Middle Ages that were to give rise to schismatic and heretical Protestantism, in company, paradoxically, with the anti-Protestant reaction of Catholics themselves, which was to be called the "Counter-Reformation", which abandoned the Bible to the Protestants. In other words, it is the most striking example of what the Spanish philosopher Ortega y Gasset brought out: by becoming fixed and frozen in opposition, one infallibly ends in copying or accentuating the very traits of what one opposes!

It is clear that Saint Teresa, in her brief fervent period of religious life in the midst of twenty years of superficiality, sought to nourish herself spiritually with the meditation so described, without getting much out of it. From that experience came her declaration that "meditation" (so understood and practiced) can be, indeed must be, a preparation for contemplative life but, paradoxically, that the latter can begin only at the moment when one feels definitively incapable of meditating . . . meditating in this sense, obviously: the only one that was known or accepted at that time!

What is Teresa going to promise us, once we have gone beyond this preliminary of the "wells"? First of all, what she calls a "water-wheel": that is, a wheel loaded with a series of buckets, which one has only to set in motion through a slight effort in order to make them come up without difficulty and pour fresh water in abundance. By that, she is designating what she herself calls the "prayer of quiet". She means by that a state of recollection in which the labor necessary to draw water from wells, considered essential for meditation, ceases: in which the imagination engages the reason in the process of reasoning, with the hope, in the end, of releasing the profound will. In fact, it seems that then the soul rests from all this buzzing by fixing its gaze peacefully on this very simple view, a view of the Christian mystery, in which, by which God begins, through his grace, to seize it, obscurely, of course, but nevertheless already consciously, by the sole fact that it surrenders and abandons itself to him. This is what seems to be implied by Teresa's own words, according to which there is no longer any activity other than that of the will, which "accepts being imprisoned by God like someone taken captive by the One who loves him".

Let us note here something that even many commentators, both believers and unbelievers, seem not to observe: from then on and in all that follows, we are as if led by the hand by one of the most astounding psychologists in the history of spirituality, but this psychology is in no way any "psychologism". It is clear from this point on that it is not simply a matter of an experience that the soul manufactures by itself, but, rather, the experience, absolutely *sui generis*, of Another, recognized on the basis of evangelical faith to be the God of Love, the God who is none other but love, who is the very Love revealed in Jesus Christ, dead and resurrected for us.

Once again, the strange inconsistency of so many commentaries, Christian or not, which go into ecstasy over the psychological feast offered by Teresa, totally unconscious of the fact that she did not care a bit about psychology and that it was God, the God of Jesus Christ, alone, in his capture of our soul, who interests her!

Let us go on, however, from the "water-wheel" to what she calls the "river" or "spring". In this third step, she tells us, our faculties themselves (memory-imagination, understanding and will) seem to go to sleep, so entirely occupied are they with God alone. This is what she depicts as "a glorious madness, a heavenly insanity, in which true wisdom is acquired, a mode of fruition in which the soul finds the greatest delight". She goes on to tell us that, at the time she wrote that, she had had this experience five or six times. It is easy to see what she is talking about here: obviously the madness of the Cross, the wisdom of God communicated in Christ dead and resurrected. In other words, this woman who undoubtedly knew only bits and pieces of Saint Paul, in translations of varying quality, was raised through her own experience to the heart of the Apostle's message.

Even beyond this experience, which one might think the highest, Teresa specifies that there is a fourth, which she likens to "rain": obviously we should understand by that those torrential rains known by Spain after periods of dryness that seem to become all-consuming. At the time, she tells us, such a union of our faculties with God is produced "that one loses one's strength almost completely in a kind of annihilation that goes hand in hand with an excessively great and sweet joy." This other state, the highest that she then knows, seems "to last at the most only half an hour".

After this first and, once again, fundamental work, which her different *Relations* would complete only in detail, she came to give, around the end of 1565, a more systematic and extensive *Way of Perfection*, striving this time to furnish her novices with a practical manual.

A first draft, in sixty-three short chapters, still remains for us, in the manuscript hand of Teresa, again in the Escorial. She herself tells us that she undertook this work at Saint Joseph's in Avila, for her religious, who wanted to have the lessons drawn from her *Life* (which at that time remained unknown outside of the few readers for whom she had intended it). This work was from the beginning encouraged once again by Bañez, who had now become her confessor. Let us note that this original version is particularly free and in a style that is often one of delightful familiarity.

During a visit to Valladolid, she was to rework it in a much more carefully composed draft, aimed at the more extensive public of her later foundations. Unfortunately, she dropped some of the most vivid illustrations of her doctrine, which modern editors have generally endeavored to restore, by inserting them more or less skillfully into the forty-two chapters of the new version.

In this final, if not definitive, form, she develops, after a preamble of three chapters, the principles of the Rule (chapters five to fifteen): mutual love, detachment, humility, remedies to apply to the minor disorders that threaten all cloisters.

A second part (which opens with the famous image of the game of chess that God plays with the soul) grapples with the question of what precisely is to be understood by contemplation: how some are incapable of it, the difficulties that one finds in it in all cases, the relationship between mental prayer and vocal prayer, and so on (chapters sixteen to twenty-six). The third part undertakes a commentary on the Our Father, admirable in both its simplicity and its depth (chapters twenty-seven to forty-two). It might be said that she gives us here, without seeming to, the idea of a type of meditation that is well within the lines of the traditional model of *lectio divina*, that is, not setting oneself against contemplation (were she supposed to be preparing for it), but orienting oneself toward it, disposing oneself for it, in order to be open when God gives it.

We should note here some new information with respect to the *Life*: she now has the prayer of quiet preceded by a prayer of recollection, in which it is again the conscious effort of the soul to surrender itself to God by simplifying itself that predominates. Naturally, it is what she now calls the "prayer of union" that concludes the whole, corresponding more or less exactly to the "rain" of the *Life*.

One should note the warlike tone of the introduction of this new volume. Teresa is now well-informed not only about the Lutheran schism but about all the troubles and oppositions that its repercussions involve all the way to Spain. For her, and this is very significant, the development of an authentic contemplative life is in the end the best weapon for combating a heresy that is based on justification by faith alone but that seriously alters the meaning and character of it.

It is the first expression of a conviction that one century later Saint Francis de Sales would make fully his own, having himself been taught not only by the experience of the controversy but also by the peaceful reconversions to the eternal Church by Protestants led back by him to the fold.

The following years were dominated by a succession of foundations, begun in 1567, which would be related by another book, specifically entitled *The Foundations*, completed by the direct testimony of her letters. She began it in 1573.

It is impossible to go into detail here about the itinerant life that these foundations involved for our contemplative, which she describes with priceless spirit, a life complicated by the clutter of her relationships, alternately profitable and disastrous, with the Bishop of Avila, the provincial, then the General of the Carmelites, and all sorts of other authorities, as many ecclesiastics as seculars (the nuncio all the way to the king included!).

The Discalced Carmelite Friars: Between John of the Cross and Gracian

All these tensions and all these troubles were brought to a climax, of course, by the foundation, in 1568, at Duruelo (in addition to the monasteries of women that did not cease to multiply) of a first monastery of Discalced Carmelite Friars, as they would be called, with, as Teresa said, "a monk and a half". The whole monk was the already venerable Antonio de Jesus, and the frail half-portion was Juan de Santo Matía, soon widely known under the name of Juan de la Cruz, who was going to become, for a time at least, her principal adviser and collaborator.

But a paradoxical incident intervened here at the highest point: the progressive replacement in this twofold role of the future saint and doctor of the Church by the amazing but how disappointing Jeronimo Gracian de la Madre de Dios.

How could Teresa, without ever breaking, strictly speaking, with her first and chief collaborator, and more than collaborator, come obviously to prefer to him, at least from the perspective of the foundations and the organization of the reformed Carmel, such a scatterbrain, the copies of whose spiritual writings betray superficiality and a pretentious vacuum on every page and who, besides which, seems to have given constant signs of a congenital and incurable weakness (not to say absence) of judgment? That is without doubt the greatest mystery of this Teresian life and work in which all is astounding but nothing at this point disconcerting.

As Marcelle Auclair says, with all her feminine delicacy, in a popular biography that is nonetheless exceptional, Teresa undoubtedly attached herself to this unfortunate as to a faithful and totally devoted, although extraordinarily incompetent, slave . . . by making him a vow of total obedience(!) —something John of the Cross certainly would have never countenanced! Especially since he would have immediately foreseen that this vow would in fact revert to a total submission of the supposed director with regard to his "directee".

Here we have the key to that peculiarity, still worse: to that true monstrosity. Teresa, as holy as she was, was one of those geniuses who do not tolerate advisers well, even the best in their eyes, if they are not always and immediately of their opinion. . . . And then, we should add, Gracian, obviously, was so amusing—what John must not have been, so subtle, so refined!—and the Madre, with all her cares, had great need of a clown in order not to explode. It is merely a shame that she made a clown her director, although she was obviously one of those women of whom Saint Francis de Sales—nevertheless—would soon say that they adore having a director . . . not at all so that he might tell them what they should do, but so that he might furnish them with good reasons to do what they have quite decided to do no matter what is said to them! . . .

If that had been all there was to it, there would not have been much harm. The trouble is that this amusing, this sparkling, this nearly crazy meddler was very good at making nearly inextricable affairs that were already sufficiently embroiled and, to say the least, would thereby place a worm in the most beautiful fruits of the founding work of the Mother.

We will return at greater leisure to Saint John of the Cross in the following chapter. Let us say here only that the beginning of the relative disagreement between him and Teresa would be a misunderstanding based on a pertinent but poorly understood criticism of a secondary point of Teresian spirituality, on which we will offer a few suggestions.

Last Teachings of Teresa

But let us return to the development of Teresa's teaching.

In 1569, Teresa composed the *Exclamaciones* to nourish the thanksgiving of her daughters after Communion. The *Conceptos del amor de Dios*, meditations on the Song of Songs,[7] were undertaken during the years when she was Prioress at the Incarnation, where she had been recalled in order to introduce her reform (in 1573). After the first nine chapters of the *Foundations*, drafted in Salamanca, *The Interior Castle* (*Las Moradas*) was begun at Toledo in 1577, finished two years later in Avila.

There we have the mature work of a spiritual ascension in which her earthly existence was going to be consumed. We must therefore pause here with even greater attention, if possible, than we paid to the doctrinal chapters of the *Vida*.

Teresa now proposes to us a schema in seven stages, which some have vainly tried to make correspond more or less to the four "waters" of the *Life*. In this supreme testimony, it is touching to find once again, transposed, the chivalric conceptions of her youth. The succession of *Moradas* (interior "mansions"), in fact, is that of a progression through the successive apartments of an enchanting castle, like that of the Grail, which is in reality the contemplative soul. She

[7] More exactly: on several well-known passages, taken separately.

would encounter Christ, her destined Bridegroom, only in the final and innermost retreats of her own interiority, in order finally to consummate her union with him in a most mysterious sanctuary. In fact, we have here an equivalent of that Eckhartian *Grunt*, or rather of the Taulerian *Abgrunt*, in which, as Augustine had already said, the soul, having arrived at the depth of itself, finally reaches, beyond itself, the direct divine encounter.

But let us look at this adventure in closer detail.

The first "mansion" is that of Christian humility: which is to say, of a self-knowledge illuminated by the example of Christ and his saints.

The second is a life in which prayer becomes the soul of all existence.

One reaches the third by concentrating on a meditation that goes hand in hand with an ultimately exemplary life. Here a fifth *Relacion* gives more detail about what is said next about the fourth mansion, namely, about the final preparation for the prayer of quiet through a prayer of recollection, which itself includes henceforth two successive stages, according to whether it is still a conscious and deliberate effort that carries it, with self-surrender to grace, or rather, already, an attraction, recognized as invincible, of that grace.

From there, one rises, or rather God himself, if he wishes, raises you to the fifth mansion, which is the prayer of quiet, now very distinct. But the latter is transcended in what Teresa calls the "spiritual betrothal", which she compares to the phase of transformation of the caterpillar in its co-coon into the butterfly that breaks free from it (the sixth mansion).

The passage from the fifth mansion, which is therefore the prayer of quiet, to the sixth is marked by interior as well as external trials, which are the final preparation for what she calls the "spiritual marriage". These trials themselves alternate at that time with extraordinary experiences, raptures, ecstasies, flights of the spirit, as she says.

Nevertheless, once the seventh and highest mansion is attained, that in which the spiritual marriage is consummated, these phenomena as well as the trials are transcended in a stable union. Then, although the consciousness of union with God in Christ no longer ceases, one finds, or rather, one acquires a freedom in action at the service of one's neighbor, and particularly in the effort to draw him toward God through the personal witness of the highest charity.

After having written this true spiritual testament, Teresa again entered into the worst trials of the Carmelite Reform, with, in 1577, the kidnapping and captivity in Toledo of the unfortunate John of the Cross by the mitigated Carmelites. The captive escaped mysteriously (miraculously?) . . . and his tormentors soon had to capitulate before the royal will.

I will pass over Gracian's dealings in that respect and over the final trials of Saint John of the Cross, for I will return to them. In 1582, we have Teresa's final journey: through Medina del Campo, Valladolid and Palencia, to her last foundation: Burgos. She returned toward Avila but had to stop at Alba de Tormes (at some distance from Salamanca), where she died of exhaustion, on October 14.

The relic of her heart has been preserved in a crystal egg. Having held it in my hands, I can certify that the wound of fire attributed to the vision of the cherubim, which Bernini's statue has questionably popularized, does indeed seem to be visible there. Belonging myself to a congregation in which there is not great enthusiasm about this kind of phenomenon, I can only note, for the dubious reader, that the same thing has been observed not only in the founder of the Oratory, Saint Philip Neri, but also in the second superior of the Oratory in France, Charles de Condren, upon whose tomb, in July, I made my prostration for priestly ordination. I apologize for these personal details: I allow myself the liberty to give them solely in order to explain why I prefer to abstain from pronouncing a judgment on these strangely "charismatic" phenomena. The final word on it might be borrowed from a contemporary: from that Shakespeare who, as Madame de Longworth-Chambrun seems indeed to have demonstrated, never abandoned the Catholic faith: "There are more things in heaven and earth . . . than are dreamt of in your philosophy . . . " (*Hamlet*, I, V).

IV

FROM TERESA TO JOHN OF THE CROSS

The Life of John of the Cross

Passing from Teresa of Avila to John of the Cross, it is necessary to begin by admitting—and clearing up—a first impression that is not easily avoidable. It is that here, as happens rather often in cases of particularly close collaboration between a man and a woman, there are moments when one no longer knows with certainty which is the man and which is the woman.[1] I mean that there is such energy in Teresa, such lucidity (when she wishes), and so uncircumventable a will that, faced with the subtlety, the delicacy, the extreme and exquisite sensitivity of John, one is sometimes tempted to see things in reverse.

In reality, if the soul of John of the Cross were a transparent crystal, one would soon have to realize that his decisions could cut like a razor. On the other hand, the extraordinary intelligence of Teresa, which made her detect as if by instinct and decisively get rid of all false pretenses, did not prevent her from being satisfied, with a wholly feminine stubbornness, with impressions. And she was capable of expressing them with such clarity that there is a great danger of not understanding that she was loath to analyze them. Sure of what she had in mind, with no concern to

[1] This is what Miguel de Unamuno has expressed with his usual vividness.

sift through the expressions she was using to say it, expressions that often came from her reading or from what she
had heard scholars say: since the latter were apparently in
agreement with her, having, once and for all, turned their
formulas to her own profit by accommodating them to her
meaning, she would stick by them!

That having been noted, one has perhaps not said everything about the conflicts between her and her "little Seneca",
but one has brought out at least the essence of it, as we shall
try to show.

Juan de Yepes, who was to become Saint John of the
Cross,[2] was born in 1542 in Fontiveros, an important village at a good fifty kilometers to the north of Avila. Even
if it is true that his father, as we are told, had blue blood in
his veins, his parents were only very modest weavers. This
father died when John was seven years old. His mother then
transported the family to Medina del Campo, a little neigh-
boring but important market town. John seems to have gone
through an astounding succession of apprenticeships: after
a carpenter, it was a tailor, then a sculptor, finally a painter
who took him in hand, before he became, at the hospital
of Medina del Campo, something like a nurse and simple
waiter.

Fortunately, he found there, in the person of a benefac-
tor of this establishment, Don Antonio Alvarez de Toledo,
a wise protector, who sent him, after elementary school, to

---

[2] The critical edition of the works of Saint John of the Cross has been provided by Father Crisógono de Jesús, in the large collection of the *Biblioteca de
autores católicos*. The most recent English translation of these works has been
provided in: *The Collected Works of Saint John of the Cross*, 2d ed. (Washington,
D.C.: Institute of Carmelite Studies, 1979). The best biography in French
remains that of Father Bruno de Jesus-Marie, O.C.D. (Paris, 1930), which
has also been published in English translation: *Saint John of the Cross* (New
York: Benziger Brothers, 1932).

the Jesuits, with the plan of making him a chaplain for the hospital. But, having reached his twentieth year, the protegé declared that he was drawn rather to Carmel.

In 1563, he was therefore admitted (under the name of John of Saint Matthias) to the Carmelites of Medina del Campo and sent by them to their college of Saint Andrew at Salamanca. We know that he remained there three years before his ordination and that he studied philosophy there rather than theology. It is suspected that he was influenced by the great humanist, poet and religious moralist (rather than theologian) Luis de Leon, to whom the edition of the works of Saint Teresa was to be entrusted. In any case, it was assuredly due to the persistence, despite the Inquisition, which was already on its guard, of the stamp of Francis de Vitoria on Salamanca, of his biblicism enlightened by a return to the Fathers of the Church, according to the inspiration of Erasmus, that John would owe his constant and profound immersion in the Bible.

In 1567, the year of his priestly ordination, probably in September, he met Teresa at Medina del Campo. At that moment, disillusioned about Carmel because of its decadence, he thought to turn toward the Carthusians. As we have seen, this meeting was going to decide a future entirely linked with the Carmelite renewal inspired, promoted, carried out toward and against all by the "Madre".

After one year of probation, on November 27, 1568, in the wise and venerable company of Antonio de Heredia— becoming Antonio de Jesus—he was himself to be, under the name of Juan de la Cruz, the beginning of the new community established (if we can use that word for such miserable beginnings) at Duruelo. Several years passed in a combination of ardent prayer and evangelization of the surrounding countryside in a nearly unbelievable poverty.

Having joined, in June of 1570, the less shabby foundation of Mancera, he became Master of Novices, transferred
in October to Pastrana. But, in the spring of 1571, he was
dispatched to found a college for the "reformed" at the University of Alcala de Henares.

In 1577, and for five years, however, he was made confessor of the women's monastery of the Incarnation at Avila,
now placed in the hands of Teresa. It was at that time that he
was going to begin his close collaboration with her, although
it very quickly became apparent that she trusted Jerome Gracian more.

Let us recall that at the height of the conflict that was going to develop with the "mitigated", on December 3, 1577,
John of the Cross was removed by the latter, transferred
to their monastery at Toledo and submitted to an infamous
captivity and treatment. It was in this jail, from which he escaped one night in August 1578 in mysterious circumstances
(which would be attributed to an intervention of the Holy
Virgin), that he would write the first thirty strophes of his
Cantico espiritual.

Taken in by the Teresian nuns of Toledo and promptly
placed in safety under the protection of a canon of the
excelentisimo cabildo of the cathedral, he was hurried from
the canon's guardianship to a friend of Carmel, Almodovar
del Campo. There, a Chapter of the "Discalced", as the
Carmelites who had returned to the primitive Rule were
called, was held in October. Unfortunately the nuncio Sega,
circumvented by the mitigated, exiled both Gracian and Antonio de Jesus. But the Chapter sent John to Monte Calvario
to substitute for the Prior, who in turn left for Rome to de-
fend the Reform.

He came and went between this monastery and the women's monastery at Beas, where he made the acquaintance

of one of the first disciples and future successor of Teresa, Ana de Jesus, and it was for this latter that he undertook the writing of a commentary for his *Canticle.*

In 1579, he founded still another college, at Baeza, and, during this stay, proceeded with poems and commentaries. The nuncio, who had become favorably disposed while all this was going on, had, in June 1581, a bull of separation, which permitted the institution of an autonomous province, delivered to Gracian.

It was in 1582 that John, a Castilian who was unenthusiastic about the Andalusian South, was nevertheless sent by the Chapter to Los Martires, near Granada, and soon was made Vicar Provincial for Andalusia.

But, in 1585, the authoritarian Doria replaced Gracian, whose incapacity had become all too evident, and obtained a complete separation of the Discalced. John was then made Prior of Segovia (head of the new Order). But Doria, not content with having eliminated Gracian, reorganized everything in a dictatorial and activist fashion. John, for having protested, was deposed by the Chapter of 1591 and sent in exile to La Peñuela. Having fallen ill in September, he was transferred for treatment to Ubeda, where he was at first persecuted by the Prior. The latter, finally, recognized his holiness. But that was nearly on the eve of John's death, which occurred on December 14 of the same year.

The Thought of John of the Cross

Let us go on to his thought and his works. We have already said that the first thirty strophes of the *Spiritual Canticle* were composed in jail in Toledo. When he escaped, he recited these to the religious who took him in.

It seems that it was shortly after this that he wrote another poem: *En una noche oscura*, in which memories of his night of escape show through. Then, in Beas, as we have noted, for Ana de Jesus in particular, he undertook the explanation of the *Canticle*. At Monte Calvario, he wrote, or at least began to write, the first two books of the commentary on the second poem, which would become the *Subida del Monte Carmelo* (*The Ascent of Mount Carmel*), and he designed the sketch representing it. The first book is limited to the first strophe of *En una noche oscura* (and even to its first words), the second jumping directly to the second. They correspond respectively to what he calls, in the first, the night of the senses (precisely: *del sentido*, which applies to all sensibility), and in the second the active night of the spirit.

Neither the end of the second book, however, nor the third that will follow is linked directly to the poem. One problem already raised by this first commentary is that it is entirely dominated, nearly exclusively taken up with the purification of the soul, while the poem was obviously permeated by its illumination from above.

Later, at Los Martires, he produced another treatise, itself entitled *La noche oscura del alma*, devoted to the passive night of the spirit, which can be considered like a fourth book added to the *Subida*.

At Baeza, moved by a reflection of a nun on the beauty of God, he added five first supplementary strophes to the *Canticle* of Toledo. Finally, it was at Los Martires again that, starting in 1581, he completed the *Spiritual Canticle* and its commentary with those of *En una noche oscura*.

A second version of the *Canticle*, despite great beauty, gives the impression of having been watered down and seems not to have been the work of John himself.[3]

[3] See Dom Chevalier, *Le Cantique spirituel de saint Jean de la Croix* (Paris,

Yet only the explanation of the *Canticle* follows the development of the poem strophe by strophe, giving the progress of the soul up to the approach of union with God.

Finally, it was at Granada, even though he was carrying out the functions of Vicar Provincial, that he produced, for his lay directee, Doña Ana de Peñalosa, the four strophes of *Llama de amor viva* (*Living Flame of Love*) and their explanation, which treat the summits of the unitive life.

It follows that, for him, what he also calls "spiritual marriage" or "unitive life" is prepared through two nights, *del sentido* and *del alma*, which both have a passive phase or aspect superimposed rather than necessarily successive to the active aspect. That is to say, in the two cases a more direct, more profound operation of God's pure grace prolongs and carries out what one had deliberately begun, though even then being helped, indeed stimulated, from above.

Let us stress that the constant movement to and fro of his commentary, always very concrete in its examination of the soul's progress, presupposes that the progression, whether from the active to the so-called passive phase or even from one night to the other, is not necessarily to be understood as a unilinear advance but as a progressive purification, proving to be increasingly effective according as grace plays a dominant role in it, although it is very clear that, far from suppressing our freedom, it puts new life into it.[4]

That is also, it seems, what explains the apparent enigma

1930). This thesis, recently rejected by the Spanish Carmelites (followed by an eminent American critic, Father Kavanaugh, O.C.D.), seems confirmed by the fact that the *Living Flame*, written toward the end of his life, remains as clear as the first *Canticle* about the anticipation of eternity already here below.

[4] This is justly brought out by Father Lucien-Marie de Saint-Joseph, O.C.D., in the introduction to his French translation of the works (Paris, 1959).

that some poems, once again wholly lit by the growing illumination of the faithful soul, become the point of departure, through the whole of the *Subida* up to the *Noche*, for
considerations directly related to the preliminary, or rather,
fundamental purification.

That seems to be equivalent to the reciprocal implication,
in Eckhart, between the *Abegescheidenheit*, ascetical detachment, and the *Gelazenheit*, pure surrender to grace.

The same observation clarifies as well the true meaning
of that "*nada*", or "nothing", which is to say, that absolute
stripping that is demanded in an uncompromising way, right
from the first words of the *Ascent of Mount Carmel*, which
is a constant preoccupation following us to the end of the
"dark night". As Father Lebreton said, in an excellent expression, with respect to the ascetical doctrine of the New
Testament itself, this ascesis must be understood, not as a
condemnation of created things, but as a preference for the
Creator, who reveals to us his love through all his creation.[5]

The *Spiritual Canticle* and, even more, the *Living Flame of
Love* show effectively that, at the summit of spiritual ascension, all created things, which one had had to pass beyond,
are found again but now become, as it were, an instrument
of praise and, for us toward the Creator as for the Creator
toward us, the reciprocal expression of a love henceforth
perfectly, equally shared.

From this, finally, comes the repeated affirmation that one
can, one should, already in this life, arrive at a true anticipation of heavenly beatitude, indeed of the final resurrection,
while all mystical experience—John would always maintain
this—is played out on the level of faith and not beyond.[6]

---

[5] Cf. Jules Lebreton, *Lumen Christi: La Doctrine spirituelle du Nouveau Testament* (Paris, 1947).

[6] See the thesis of Karol Wojtyła, *Doctrina de Fide apud Sanctum Johannem
a Cruce* (Rome, 1949) (English translation: *Faith according to Saint John of the*

This is indeed what is implied by the twofold aspect of John's "nights", which we have pointed out from the beginning of Spanish mysticism: a dark night, in which all seems to fade away from earthly realities, but a blessed night, at the height of which a union is consummated that precedes the dawn through its fullness and certitude.

Origin of the Doctrine of Saint John of the Cross

In order to go more deeply into this apparent paradox, one must enter farther into the manner in which Saint John of the Cross carries out his theological systematization of mystical experience. But, even before that, it is essential to weigh the entire understanding that the first (and, in a sense, ultimate) expression has of this experience: in poems, and very particularly in that sublime poetry, if there ever was such, of John of the Cross. Here awaits us, curiously, what a purely philosophical analyst like Jean Baruzi,[7] and even more a critic, who claims to be simply literary, like Damaso Alonso,[8] seem to have perceived much better, not only than theologians too zealous to adjust the straitjacket of their concepts to him, but also than spiritual masters themselves, who wish to recognize in him only wholly timeless inspiration. For it was not by chance that John of the Cross expressed his mysticism first of all in poems and, one would be tempted to say, wholly expressed it only in that way.

Cross [San Francisco: Ignatius Press, 1981]): the last six paragraphs of the first chapter.

[7] Cf. Baruzi, *Saint Jean de la Croix et le problème de l'expérience mystique* (Paris, 1924), 305ff. His vision of the importance here of the poetic expression in no way justifies, however, his attempt to reduce mysticism to a purely metaphysical experience.

[8] Cf. Damaso Alonso, *La Poesia de San Juan de la Cruz* (Madrid, 1958).

In poetry, in fact, he did not have merely a refined talent like that of Hadewijch: his poetry, in the opinion of the best experts, is perhaps the purest and most elevated of its kind ever produced in Spain, and when one knows the place of Spanish literature, and especially of its poetry, in the forefront of all the literatures of Europe and America, it is worth the effort to pause here.

For, more than any philosophy, or even theology, poetry of this quality, of this order, can be considered as the propaedeutic par excellence for mysticism, and especially for Christian mysticism, if one really wants to approach the latter by way of what Lebreton has told us of his asceticism, once again done not from condemnation but from preference. Not that one need intermingle, or merely confuse, poetry and mysticism, as Henri Bremond did. But a poem, by making us recognize in this world an image of the invisible, an echo of the creative word, is precisely what incites us, at the height of the recognition of all its beauty, to progress farther: to open ourselves, to respond with all our being, to give our living faith to the One who speaks in this way.

Whether or not John of the Cross followed the courses of Luis de Leon at Salamanca is secondary. It was enough to live there at that time in order to breathe this so-called "pastoral" Spanish poetry, illustrated, among others, by Boscan, whom Luis and Juan would imitate, each in his turn, but who is a rediscovery of the meaning and inseparability of untouched nature and a human love carried to the maximum of intensity as well as of purity. And, for a soul that was as artistic and vibrant as his own, the Erasmian humanist discovery of the Bible (which did not burst forth just at that moment by chance) was both to be enlightened by this cultural renewal and to illuminate it in return.

For the biblical word is not the word of a professor but an

essentially poetic word, in the sense of being creative and re-creative: the word of the "Living One who gives life", of Love par excellence, who calls all to love what He loves, as He loves, by loving it Himself first, before all, above all, but also finally in all being, in everything.

That, without a doubt, is the proper place of all Saint John of the Cross' inspiration—I do say all: not indistinctly, to be sure, but inseparably: poetic, biblical and, in the end, mystical.

It can be considered providential that the technical, university element of his Salamanca education, with this very particular culture in which it had steeped him, had exercised his mind only in the philosophical dialectic, which would become the simple implement of a very finely tuned discernment. As for the school of theology, at the period when he was a student there—thank God he had only slight contact with it! Under the influence of Inquisitorial reaction, far from tracing Saint Thomas back to his proper sources, the Bible and the Fathers, even his most faithful disciples, like Bañez, and even worse, of course, someone like Melchior Cano (the anti-mystic par excellence), imagined that they were protecting the divine, Christian mystery, not by situating it precisely, not by articulating it, like the Angelic Doctor had done, but by choking it with an enthusiastic dialectic that thought to explain it, justify it, extend it, while it tended only to dissipate it. Let us think of what would happen a little later with John of Saint Thomas (wholly incontestable genius that he was): of a theology that imagined it was able to extend revelation in some way, without taking into account that it was thus flooding it in an a priori philosophy wholly constructed previously at the outset from faith, and, pretending to develop it, reduced it in a way to a system of a rationality that was nothing but human.

Providentially avoiding these digressions and traps, the spiritual theology of Saint John of the Cross, intrinsically theological by the very fact that it is constructed wholly from spirituality, and remaining at the heart of the latter, would be a theology solely of *agapē*, of "the love of God poured into our hearts by the Spirit who has been given us", as Saint Paul says. But, for all that, a theology of the Cross, following Saint John the Evangelist, it will also be, at the same stroke, a theology of the Resurrection and Ascension: that is to say, of the full assumption of man in God, by a communion with the God made man of our fallen humanity, who will raise it up again and exalt it to the very bosom of the Father.

And it is that which finally gives us the key to that very categorical affirmation of John of the Cross: As authentic an anticipation as it may be of eternal life, mystical contemplation, with that mysticism wholly stemming from the mystery of the Cross, is not on the level of the beatific vision but remains at the level of faith.

But how is this to be understood? On this point, despite his regrettable immersion in late Scholasticism, in particular in a "John-of-Saint-Thomas" substitute for the Thomism of Thomas, Jacques Maritain must be recognized for the merit of having put his finger on the focal point. Namely, that if the God of Christian contemplation is love, and if his very love is given us, we have there a super-eminent case of that dark but sure knowledge that Saint Thomas calls "knowledge of connaturality".[9] It is in this sense, following a tradition that goes back to Saint Gregory the Great through William of Saint Thierry, that one can say that it is love itself that, in those who are possessed by it, produces know-

---

[9] Cf. Jacques Maritain, *Distinguer pour unir ou Les Degrés du savoir* (Paris, 1948), 515ff.

ledge: *amor est intellectus*.[10] Not that it need be understood as if love itself became knowledge, which is pure nonsense, but, quite simply, following the words of Saint Paul, one comes to know God as one has been known: that is, one knows him as loving by loving, with his own love having taken a total possession of our heart.

There we touch what is truly the nerve of the clarification, of the necessary corrections brought by John of the Cross to the work, as inspired as it is, of Teresa. The principal one is certainly in this capacity of his, as a cleric, to benefit from the return to the sources brought about by the best Christian humanism, which was nearly immediately closed to laymen in general, and to women in particular, by the vigilance of the Inquisition with regard to the *alumbrados*. These latter had, however, been influenced as much and more by medieval heresies than by Lutheranism, but it was the insistence of Luther on the Bible that motivated the insistence on the rejection of all biblical popularization.

In this perspective, it is certainly lamentable to note the sure instinct that urged Teresa to return to the Gospels and, more generally, to the entire word of God, as the primary source of inspiration. It is equally lamentable to note the material barriers that obstructed her way as well as that of all women religious of her day who had received the education judged proper to women: quite simply ignorance of Latin along with a lack of in-depth understanding of the liturgical tradition.

John of the Cross, on the contrary, as Jean Vilnet[11] has very precisely established, was nourished on the Bible read as a whole, ceaselessly reread, meditated upon according to

---

[10] On the problems raised by the interpretation of this formula, see J. Déchanet, *Aux sources de la spiritualité de Guillaume de Saint-Thierry* (Bruges, 1940), 18ff.

[11] Jean Vilnet, *Bible et mystique chez Saint Jean de la Croix* (Paris, 1945).

the organic development of its major themes. The excellent index furnished by Father Lucien-Marie de Saint-Joseph to his translation would be almost enough in itself to convince us of this. It was on the basis, or rather in the rootedness, of this biblicism that the critical lucidity, aroused in John by his philosophical studies, was going to lead him either to correct Teresa's affirmations or to contradict them purely and simply.

On the first point, yielding to the profound holiness of a spirituality wholly absorbed in the passionate search for the encounter, the consummated union with God in Christ, the latter accepted, indeed desired, in the first stages of her spiritual progress, visions, locutions and all other extraordinary phenomena that can be so many marks of divine grace taking possession of one's whole being, although she might have fundamentally agreed in thinking and saying that all this would be transcended, put aside, forgotten, so to speak, in the spiritual marriage.[12]

John, on the other hand, with his direct critical perception of the essence, would maintain that one must neither desire such graces nor even pause, even in passing, at their gift, even if authentic, for he perceived too well, from the very fact of the intensity of his poetic sensibility, the danger of attachment, of sinking, of idolatry, in short, that can represent all that is not God, God alone, loved for himself alone.[13]

His opposition is there aimed simply at a feminine sensibility that is naturally inclusive and certainly supremely attached to the essential but that perceives the latter only in all its reverberations, without bothering about speculative dis-

[12] Cf. the first three chapters of the seventh mansion, in the *Interior Castle*.
[13] A text like chapter 16 of the second book of the *Subida del Monte Carmelo* leaves no doubt about his judgment.

tinctions between the envelope and its contents, the hearth
and its heat. And when the conflict goes farther, it seems
indeed that it is rather one concerning words than realities.

I would like to speak here of the rejection, which was
certainly formal on John's part, of Teresa's assurance that
spiritual marriage, in her case, was accompanied by an intellectual (but singularly concrete!) vision of Christ always
present at her side and, much more, of the Trinity itself.
John considers such things to be equally impossible at this
stage. He is certain that these expressions, on the lips or
from the pen of Teresa, merely repeat formulas found in
books or suggested by her confessors (in this case, probably Bañez) and to which she was attached, not because they
were important to her in themselves but because she found
in them a justification for certitudes inseparably linked to
her experience.

Nevertheless, John of the Cross himself certainly never
wanted to reject what was equally close to his heart: that
spiritual marriage was lived as a union of ourselves with
God in Jesus Christ, Son of God made flesh, and that in
consequence of this union we are introduced into the trinitarian life itself: this unity of a transcendent love on which
Eckhart and his disciples as well as Ruusbroec insisted, each
in more or less varied formulas, following Hadewijch.

We can conclude our sketch in no better way, in this regard, than with a quotation from the *Cantico* and another
from the *Llama*, with their respective commentaries. This
certitude of participating in exchanges of love between the
three Divine Persons is affirmed there as the final word of
Saint John of the Cross on the union consummated between
the soul and the Son of God who became man, as the Fathers say, "in order to make us gods".

> The breathing of the air,
> The song of the sweet nightingale,
> The grove and its living beauty
> In the serene night,
> With a flame that is consuming and painless . . .

This breathing [*aspirar*] of the air is an ability [*habilidad*]
which the soul states God will give her there in the communication of the Holy Spirit. By His divine breath-like spira-
tion [*aspirar*], the Holy Spirit elevates the soul sublimely and
informs her and makes her capable of breathing in God the
same aspiration of love that the Father breathes in the Son
and the Son in the Father, which is the Holy Spirit Himself,
Who in the Father and the Son breathes out to her in this
transformation, in order to unite her to Himself.[14]

And here from the *Living Flame*:

> O sweet cautery,
> O delightful wound!
> O gentle hand! O delicate touch
> That tastes of eternal life
> And pays every debt!
> In killing You changed death to life.

In this stanza the soul proclaims how the three Persons of
the Most Blessed Trinity, the Father, the Son, and the Holy
Spirit, are they Who effect in it this divine work of union.
Thus the hand, the cautery, and the touch are substantially
the same. The soul applies these terms to the Persons of the
Trinity because of the effect each of the Persons produces.
The cautery is the Holy Spirit; the hand is the Father; and

---

[14] *Cancion* 39 of the *Cantico espiritual* and its explanation. In English translation: *The Collected Works*, 557–58.

the touch is the Son. The soul here magnifies the Father, the Son, and the Holy Spirit, stressing the three admirable favors and blessings they produce in it, having changed its death to life, transforming it in the Trinity.[15]

[15] *Cancion* 2 of the *Llama* and its explanation. In English translation: *The Collected Works*, 595.

V

THÉRÈSE OF LISIEUX

Three Carmelites for Our Times

In passing from John of the Cross to Thérèse of Lisieux, we arrive at a trio of modern Carmelites, all three in a Teresian and Sanjuanist tradition, each very different from the others but admirably complementary, of whom one can say that their providential conjunction is indeed a "sign of the times", if this can be said for these recent times that are ours.

They have done more than anyone else to make it possible for Christians to lead, either in the cloister or in the world, a contemplative life of a Christian purity and intensity seldom seen since the patristic period. It is to their remarkable credit that they represent a progressive return to the sources not only with precision and striking determination but also, through their example as well as through the written testimony they have left us, with a universal approach.

Here, with these three feminine figures, it can truly be said that we encounter that sense of the real that is so feminine along with an inborn pedagogical talent that, again, women alone seem capable of demonstrating. That these three are found in the same Carmelite order in our time, succeeding each other from one generation to the next, can be considered one of the greatest heavenly gifts made to the Church at a time when a weakened Christianity has had more need of it than ever . . . and, in truth!, has scarcely seemed to deserve it.

What is most remarkable about the first two is that nothing, either in their family circles or even less in their immediate "religious" surroundings, seemed to have prepared them for so exceptional a vocation.

No less striking is the fact that the third came to the faith only as an adult, from an orthodox and very respectable, faithful Judaism, although she seemed in her own eyes, quite wrongly, moreover, to have strayed from her entire heritage.

These two little (very little!) bourgeois French women, this German of fine Jewish tradition, but apparently indifferent to the faith of her ancestors, would certainly do more, through the succession of their lives and their works, than all the most celebrated men of the Church in their century—imposing ecclesiastics, fervent missionaries or brilliant theologians—to regenerate an anemic Christianity.

Thérèse of the Child Jesus and of the Holy Face

In coming without further delay to the one whom we call today Saint Thérèse of Lisieux, we must admit that the enormous literature to which she has given rise is, with very few exceptions, more discouraging than inspiring. When I say that, I must immediately add that I am lumping together both a cheaply constructed creation of which Lisieux was for too long the center and the anti-Martin and/or anti-Carmelite productions that so many camouflages and all that saccharine were inevitably to arouse in return. When one has compared the authentic texts of Thérèse with the Lisieux transcriptions, one may be tempted to some bad temper with respect to the too-famous Carmel and to the honorable Martin family that colonized it. But, coming back to views not only more merciful but quite simply more realistic, it is only to be plunged either into the unbalanced imaginations of some

literary man or, worse still, the fantasies of some psycho-
analyst of the sacristy.

To tell the truth, in what concerns the family in question,[1] the mother, who was a glutton for work, and the father, who, on the other hand, was born to be a person of
leisure (and was, moreover, very shrewd in his investments),
but, apart from that, very good, God-fearing, right-minded
people, reflect the sentimental piety, nourished with plati-
tudes, that is characteristic of their whole period. But the
least one can do is to recognize them as capable of generosity that one would like to find more common among the
"militants" of our own time, when people believe themselves (Catholics first of all) so much more enlightened!

As for this Carmel that would increasingly tend to be or
to seem, in the years that were to follow, only an ectoplasm
of the aforementioned family, one must believe that, in any
case, before the "little flower" had become an exceptional
"boom", one could undoubtedly be sanctified there, since
this happened to Thérèse, even if hygiene was nonexistent
there—taste: let us not speak of it!—and despite the approx-
imate observance and the, on the whole, rather mediocre
personnel. To begin with, there was a whimsical superior,
steeped in herself, but not so bad a woman nor so mediocre

---

[1] On Thérèse, the main source is obviously the *Manuscrits autobiographiques*,
edited by Father François de Sainte-Marie in 1956 (English trans.: *Story of
a Soul* [Washington, D.C.: Institute of Carmelite Studies, 1972]), to which
must be added the *Derniers entretiens* published in 1971 (English trans.: *St.
Thérèse of Lisieux: Her Last Conversations* [Washington, D.C.: Institute of
Carmelite Studies, 1977]). We have greatly benefited from the book by Hans
Urs von Balthasar, *Schwestern im Geist: Therese von Lisieux und Elisabeth von Dijon* (Einsiedeln: Johannes Verlag, 1970), English translation: *Two Sisters in the
Spirit* (San Francisco: Ignatius Press, 1992) and also from two works by Msgr.
Guy Gaucher, O.C.D., *Histoire d'une vie: Thérèse Martin* (Paris: Cerf, 1986),
and *La Passion de Thérèse de Lisieux* (Paris: Cerf, 1973). It goes without saying
that I am alone responsible for the reflections with which these various texts
inspired me.

a religious as has been assumed, since she did not hesitate
to give (if not confiding completely, but one must not ask
too much!) a responsibility like that of the novitiate to a
child who was obviously richly gifted but whose sanctity,
nonetheless, was not immediately revealed.

What is a marvel about Thérèse is that, born and brought
up in this family, certainly of good Christians but with so
poor an education both on the religious plane and on the
plane of simple humanity, formed, if the word can be applied, in a cloistered life that seems even more banal still,
she was able to develop so healthy a spirituality and to give
so quickly a teaching of it that was so accurately oriented
to the essential.

The milieu into which she was born, and her mother
in particular, have been accused of having developed and
communicated to her children a "death instinct".[2] Let us
greet, under a Freudian mask, one of those ecclesiastics of
all times in the style of the priest Eli, who, seeing a woman
pray with particular fervor, could only deduce that she was
deranged if not simply alcoholic! (1 Sam 1:9-14).

In fact, a wholly clerical insensibility is necessary to call
by this name the spirit of faith and sacrifice that allowed this
woman, herself soon removed from her family, to preserve
for herself and to inculcate in them so tranquil a courage in
the face of a succession of infant deaths and then in the face
of a fatal illness to which she had to submit with a simplicity
that such priests should envy in such laymen!

As for Thérèse, a difficult character, a spoiled child, coddled by a mother's, father's and sisters' adoration, the Christianity she received from those around her could well be expressed in intolerable language and could be overburdened
with practices (not a Jansenist Christianity, as is everlastingly

---

[2] We prefer not to give the reference for this pedantic absurdity.

repeated to us, but much rather a naïvely Pelagian one, in its accumulation of good works posted in the account books), yet it did not forget that love was to be the soul of it: otherwise how would she grasp so soon and retain forever the fact that love was worth more than all the rest?

Let us add to this, first of all, the illnesses of the child, which denote an organic fragility, undoubtedly not unrelated to her hypersensitivity, but also a precocious intelligence that would help her free herself and which, taking into account the meager intellectual resources of these surroundings, was not, all the same, prevented from developing there; rather, quite the contrary seems to have been the case. The worst thing for which one can reproach this family milieu is for having nourished so much sentimentality, so great a lack of taste that it gave rise to the idea of presenting, through insane alterations, like that of a sickeningly sweet, insipid doll, a face of Thérèse that would seem almost vulgar, by sheer force of its stubborn will, if it were not saved by the splendor of its gaze.

But what compels more reflection is, not that one finally manages to rediscover the true Thérèse and extract her from all this sugar, but that so many of the simplest, honest people so quickly scented the truth, the reality, beneath these dubiously celestial perfumes. Certainly, among the devotees of the "little Thérèse", there are and will still for a long time be those unrepentant idolaters who prefer the caricature to the unretouched portrait! But what has long struck me, like many others, well before the discovery of the true portrait and the true writings, are the many simple people who, by instinct, disregarding, not even noticing this disguise, went straight to the essential: the unique gospel authenticity of her "little way", revealing to them, by her example more than by her own words, whether untouched or censored, what Saint Augustine himself had so magnificently expressed for the most learned by saying to God: "*Da quod jubes, et jube quod vis*"—"You need only give yourself what you order, and you will indeed be able to order whatever you wish!"

The strange Bremond, who, with all the appearances of a poor priest, was capable of such good judgment and was not fooled himself for an instant!

Complete faith leading to (or rather discovering itself within) commitment, head bowed, in a night without stars: this was what was of value in her, sensed rather than perceived, from the start and ceaselessly, in every setting, by devout people who did not even notice the gilded paper garlands that had been used to dress up the most naked, the most apparently devastated "*fiat*", but one that was already under the whole weight of the most certainly triumphant Cross.

Yet, let us go a little into the details of this life, so soon surrendered, so soon interrupted, but already consummated.

If there was a positive value in her family religion, despite the all-too-evident lacks and despite even the cult of which Thérèse was the object from her very earliest age, it was undoubtedly generosity in the service of God as well as in that of neighbor. If there may have been a dolorist coloring around this element, in the conventional idiom of the piety inherited from Romanticism, it appears that it was rather a matter of language (an exasperating language, to be sure) than a true distortion. Once again, to speak, particularly with respect to Thérèse's mother, of a "death instinct", as some have stupidly done, must be with an unconscious but gloomy irony, when one thinks of the succession of infant deaths that must have darkened the family atmosphere, then of the illness and relatively premature death of the mother in question!

Rather, what seems true is that her spirit of sacrifice was what allowed her, as well as her surviving children, to endure these blows without in any way being engulfed by despair. And what is there to say of the slow agony of the father, which was going to begin just at the time Thérèse entered religious life?

In any case, we cannot even say that Thérèse, for her part, had to free her sacrificial spirit from any dolorism whatever: we find no indication that she ever had need to do so!

With her mother dead, however, her childhood, coddled more than ever by her older sister Pauline,[3] would be marked by the brief, serious and still undefined illness to which we have alluded, from which she would recover with surprising speed after a very special supplication by her and her family to the Virgin. The experience would remain for her one of a smile observed on the statue in her room.

It is possible to see in this a first sign of her vocation, in the feeling of belonging henceforth to the heavenly Mother who had given her life.

Nevertheless, the following years saw her still passing through a crisis of scruples, undoubtedly important if not decisive, in order to prompt her to look, not so much at herself, as at God. Pauline's entrance into Carmel, in any case, even if it gave rise to another crisis, prepared the way for the resolution of it by hastening the conviction of her own vocation. But it is necessary to stress: in spite of the fact that all her sisters, one after the other, would become religious, even if not all Carmelites in Lisieux, it was certainly not for Thérèse the desire to find there once again the sister who was closest to her that determined her to follow

[3] Let us give a little more information about Thérèse's siblings. The oldest sister was Marie-Louise, who was her godmother, the first to enter the Carmel of Lisieux (Sister Marie of the Sacred Heart), then Marie-Pauline (Mother Agnes of Jesus), Marie-Léonie, finally settled, after many hesitations, at the Visitation Convent at Caen (Sister Françoise-Thérèse), Marie-Céline last (Sister Geneviève of the Holy Face). Marie-Helène, Marie-Mélanie-Thérèse, Joseph-Louis and Joseph-Jean-Baptiste died as small children.

her example: on the contrary, right from the beginning and
all the way to her own end, she would be very conscious
of the danger of giving in, as little as may be, to such sentimental considerations.

Finally, it was following a pilgrimage to Rome, in the
company of her father, after an audience with Leo XIII,
that she obtained permission, though not without local resistance, to enter this Carmel at the age of only fifteen years.

Soon struck down by tuberculosis, treated too late or
poorly, she was to die in 1897, at twenty-four years, after
a novitiate in which it can hardly be argued that, through
her eagerness for the divine word and the extraordinarily
keen understanding that she was to develop, she was her
own best, indeed her only true, mistress. One must at least
recognize this merit in those who should have played this
role: that they more or less clearly realized this, sufficiently
in any case to have more than half confided to her the task
that should have been their own.

It is to this paradoxical situation, vaguely sensed by both
the old Prioress, Mother Marie de Gonzague and her own
sister Pauline, who alternated with the former in this function (under the name, now, of Mother Agnes), that we owe
the complex production and publication, as early as 1898, of
what would be entitled *Histoire d'une âme* [*Story of a Soul*].

From Histoire d'une âme
to the Écrits autobiographiques

Almost immediately, the success of this volume was extraordinary. Once again, Bremond has the rare merit of being one
of the first to see some of the profound reasons that justified
this success.

This publication was in fact a synthesis and a revision

(what is sometimes called today a "rewriting") of three texts by Thérèse, through the care of Mother Agnes (alias Pauline Martin).

The first text, originally entitled *Histoire d'une petite fleur blanche* [Story of a little white flower](!), had been written at the request of Mother Agnes from January 1895 to January 1896, which is to say, when the first signs of what was soon to be recognized as tuberculosis led them to believe that Thérèse would not live much longer. The second is a long letter (of ten pages) addressed to Sister Marie of the Sacred Heart (another Martin sister, the first to enter Carmel, Thérèse's godmother). Finally, in 1897, Mother Marie de Gonzague, Prioress at the time of Thérèse's novitiate, and who had become Prioress again after Mother Agnes' term of office, had, at the request of the latter, told Thérèse to go on with this autobiography beginning with her entrance to the Carmel (where the first document had stopped).

All this together was what Mother Agnes blended and touched up in such a way that the whole would appear to be a single block of text addressed, from one end to the other, to Mother Marie de Gonzague.

It was necessary to wait for the death of Mother Agnes (in July 1951) before there could be any question of going back to the original documents. Father François de Sainte-Marie finally published the whole in facsimile in 1956.[4]

Three fundamental points emerge from this, particularly stressed by Hans Urs von Balthasar and precisely developed and clarified by Msgr. Guy Gaucher, O.C.D., in his excellent biography. These three main points are the vocation to Love, the "little way" and the experience of a darkening of faith in her final days. We will examine them, using the

---

[4] The text of this was published by Éditions du Seuil as a pocketbook edition, *Le Livre de vie*.

original texts as our basis, with particular reference to these
two authors.

Love, Little Way and Darkness of Faith

Obviously the most fundamental point of the spirituality
that Thérèse proposes to us is what she recognized as her
own vocation, in meditating on the great Pauline text of
1 Corinthians 12 and 13: on the different "charisms" and
different "ministries" of the various members of that Body
of Christ that is the Church. Faced with these directly apostolic charisms that are all dominated by charity and to the
service of charity, Thérèse wonders to which she can herself be called. She concludes that, insofar as she is a contemplative, her particular charism is, if one can say so, not of
having but of dedicating herself, directly and totally, to the
love that is itself the end and driving force for all of them.
This Love, the *agapē* of the New Testament, the proper love
of God poured into our hearts by the Spirit that has been
given us, according to the expression of chapter five of Ro-
mans, thus appears to be, as it were, what must make contemplation itself the soul of any apostolate. She finds in it
what justifies her entering Carmel, understood, in principle
and, more and more, formally, not as disinterest with regard
to a sinful world and its salvation, but, on the contrary, as
both the most spiritual way and the most realistic way of
contributing to it.

From that will come, each in its turn, the concrete way by
which she will surrender herself to love in this perspective
and the price that her attainment, her achievement will cost
her in the final analysis. This will be, first of all, the "little
way", as she said, which Mother Agnes (for once not so
ill-inspired) was to rebaptize the "way of childhood", for

there is no doubt that Thérèse understood it as total filial abandonment to the Father, in union with his Son, in a fundamentally evangelical perspective.[5]

Thérèse seems to have had a presentiment of it very early: when she said that she was to be like a ball in the hands of the Child Jesus, so that he might do as he wished, toss it where and when he pleased. The little Thérèsian way is, in fact, to bestow oneself so fully to the Father in his Son that he may make of us what he wishes, as he wishes, counting simply but absolutely on him to give us, along with light on what we must do at every moment, the strength to consent to it and to accomplish it, without any resistance or hesitancy.

Yet the experience of physical suffering, the certitude that it was soon going to lead to death, were accompanied in her, in the very consent that she gave to it, by a true anticipated experience of the Resurrection: for the Resurrection not only always follows the Cross, but it is found implicit within it, at least when the Cross is that of Christ in us. This is what would be for Thérèse, in the supreme period of her accomplishment in her blind surrender to Love, the source of an unflinching faith. The latter was exercised in the acceptance of all the sufferings, as they presented themselves, at the moment when they presented themselves and up to the most demanding: not a loss but a darkening of faith. Her faith then continued to exist, it survived, it triumphed in the perseverance, in the absolutism of the one love in the darkest of nights.

In all of this, provided that it is placed in the perspective in which Thérèse lived, one sees clearly that it was neither

---

[5] It has been justly brought out that Thérèse frequently addresses God by calling him "Papa", just as the early Christians, following the example of Jesus, said "Abba".

dolorism nor any complacency, any attraction for suffering in itself: she simply accepted it, as the purification necessitated by love, which is, in short, the essence of all.

In this regard, the *Derniers entretiens* [*Last Conversations*], in the sense in which Msgr. Gaucher has so faithfully commented on them,[6] are decisive: it was in the darkening of her faith, through insurmountable doubts, prolonged up to the ultimate moment of her agony, and from which she seemed to leave only in leaving this present life, in the light of a supreme illumination that coincided with her consummated death, that she would attain the consummation of pure love in a totally naked faith.

Concurrently with this entry into the mystery of saving love through totally abandoned faith what one can call the intrinsically missionary character of her contemplative vocation was developed, concretized within her. More particularly, she experienced it as the meaning of the Carmelite vocation: to pray and suffer, to pray in suffering, to make her suffering a prayer because one suffers through love and in love. She understood it very soon as a vocation in support of the apostolic priesthood. But also, and first of all, it is necessary to recognize and understand that, from its first form, her vocation, so closely linked to the idea of lifting up a fallen priest, the strayed Carmelite Hyacinthe Loyson, better still of leading back to God at the last moment the criminal Pranzini, was a vocation of "compassion", in the most precise sense: for and with sinners. It is thus that Christ, in making himself one with sinners in the darkness of their very sin, saved them by continuing to love divinely, to the height of a desolation pushed farther than all that anyone has ever known. To associate oneself, therefore, with Christ

---

[6] In his volume: *La Passion de Thérèse de Lisieux*.

to the extreme point of his "My God, my God, why hast thou abandoned me?" is really to participate in the redemption by participating in the love that is the soul of it, in its integrity. For all that, it is to plunge without doubt into a night more profound even than the dark night of faith such as John of the Cross evoked it.

But that is only the ultimate end of the "little way", and it is in this way that she reaches a communion with those very ones who could be called the anticipated damned, that she rejoins them right where Jesus rejoined them, in the fullness of the divine love incarnated in the very flesh of sin. It is peculiar that this unquestionable doctrine (and first of all this experience) of Thérèse could disconcert a theologian as profound and also as subtle as Hans Urs von Balthasar.[7] Is this not just exactly what he himself was able to present, following Adrienne von Speyr, as the meaning of the descent into hell on Holy Saturday? Nevertheless, he could not recognize this meaning of the Sanjuanist night we have indicated, which is so positive in the final analysis, in the suffering, dying Thérèse, desolate but faithful up to the end in following Christ everywhere he went here below. He was right in one sense and wrong at the same time.

He was right, I would say, for in very virtue of this ultimate degree of union of the little Carmelite to her Bridegroom of blood, which goes to the point of sharing in his own dereliction, one is beyond the pure mystical experience envisaged by John of the Cross. But what von Balthasar seems not to have seen is that this experience is transcended as mystical experience, in the usual sense of the word, in its individual subjectivity: she is opened, enlarged beyond

---

[7] See Hans Urs von Balthasar, *Two Sisters in the Spirit* (San Francisco: Ignatius Press, 1992), pp. 340ff.

all limits, to the dimensions of this communion, which was that of Christ on the Cross, in the very darkness of sin. From this comes what one can call a properly saving experience, an experience of love humiliated to the very degree that it is saving. If the word "co-redemption" can have any meaning, it is only if such a possibility exists for the Christian to unite himself in such a way to Christ already here on earth. It is true that one could not conceive of it except as an antechamber to death, a death that nevertheless introduces one directly to the resurrection. But that is indeed an eminent realization of that "common life", in the sense in which Ruusbroec took it, that goes beyond, that opens contemplation itself onto a total immersion of the believer in the saving charity of the Savior.

The Gospel of the Father
and the Mystery of the Cross

Following the lead of the better commentators, we have begun by bringing out what one might call the logic, the internal coherence of the development, the flowering in Thérèse's soul of her experience and the spiritual message to our time that is not distinguishable from it. But it is important to see that this structure is revealed only progressively to Thérèse herself. That will lead us at the same time toward a more precise appreciation of this return to the Gospels, attained in what Saint Paul (just like the Gospel of Mark) calls "the Mystery", a return, or rather a renewal, of the entire Christian spirituality that one must not hesitate to attribute to Thérèse. For her part, there is no doubt that she would speak rather, quite simply, of coming back, of entering again into the Heart, without suspecting that this is to define the whole plan of that axial line of development of Eastern Orthodoxy called "hesychasm", or, more simply, the "Jesus Prayer".

In fact, the first main intuition of what one might call her spirituality, but which is only a rediscovery of the most fundamental Christian spiritual tradition, is her "little way".

Here is how she begins by defining it, then the most profound implications that she would express first.[8]

At the end of 1894, the beginning of 1895, after six years of Carmelite life, she questions herself. She has become aware of her own incapacity to attain the holiness for which she had chosen Carmel. But this discovery, far from discouraging her, only succeeds in occasioning a wholly new sudden awareness: it is not up to her to arrive at holiness: it is God, in Jesus Christ, who alone can and wishes to lead her to it. From this comes the immediate conclusion: the whole thing is to abandon oneself to him, to him alone, but totally, at every moment.

Let us note here, with Msgr. Gaucher, that the situation was still the same at that time in Carmel as it had been in the time of Saint Teresa of Avila: it was unthinkable that a Carmelite would have a Bible at her disposal. (Thérèse would succeed in having a complete, or nearly complete, New Testament only by having the Gospels along with the Epistles bound for herself by one of her sisters still in the world!)[9] But this sister, Céline, before coming to the monastery in her turn, had had the good fortune to copy, at the home of their uncle and aunt Guérin, who themselves, strangely enough, possessed a Bible in French, some texts from the Old Testament that had struck her. Thérèse threw herself on this nourishment. And it was thanks to

[8] I refer to *Histoire d'une vie: Thérèse Martin*, 147 ff.

[9] See the introduction by Msgr. Guy Gaucher to *La Bible avec Thérèse de Lisieux* (Paris, 1979).

these providential notes of Céline that she first came to lo-
cate this text from chapter 9 of Proverbs: "If anyone is very
little, let him come to me!" Without a doubt, she immediately said to herself, reading it in the state of mind we have
just described: it is to me that this is addressed! "Then", she
will cry out, "I have come!"

But another question posed itself to her: "What is God
going to do with me now?" In the same notes, it was thus that
she came across these verses from Isaiah 66: "As a mother
caresses her child, so will I console you, I will carry you at
my breast, I will rock you on my knees." She herself noted
her immediate reaction: "Oh, my God, you have surpassed
my expectations, and I, I want to sing your mercies!" (Let
us note the very characteristic fact: her response itself is a
Psalm verse. . . .)

Henceforth, the "little way", which, as we noted before,
her sister very rightly termed the "way of childhood", has
been found. Of course she did not proceed from these two
verses of the Old Testament, taken out of context, but from
the light that they are able, taken together, to cast on what
we would readily say is most evangelical in the entire gospel.

In other words, the Thérèsian "little way" is simply the
logic of Saint Paul's justification by faith, understood as Saint
Thomas Aquinas himself understood it: that is, a justification by faith *alone*,[10] not in that heretical sense into which
Luther, enraged by an uncomprehending polemic, was to
fall: as if man had nothing more to do, could remain just
as he is since he has faith, but indeed in the sense given by
Saint Paul himself: "I can do all things through him who
strengthens me",[11] responding in a way to the affirmation

---

[10] Cf. Saint Thomas Aquinas, *In Galatas*, especially lesson IV (on chapter III).

[11] Phil 4:13.

of the Savior himself, transmitted by Saint John: "Outside of me, you can do nothing!"[12]

This will explain why Thérèse has been able to convert Protestants, like that Pastor Grant, of the Presbyterian Church of Scotland, who had a vision of her and whose widow—an exquisite old lady called home to God not very long ago—was until her death the caretaker of the house in which Thérèse was born, in Alençon. Let us add that all Protestants who are truly believers and of good faith whom I know, if they have read these pages in the *Histoire d'une âme*, are persuaded at least that a Catholic saint was able to express and practice what they consider to be the best of their religion. Without dwelling too long here on this Thérèsian ecumenism, let us say that this is the best example of the fact that simple fidelity to what they believe most positively, provided it is sufficiently lucid and generous, is still, on the part of Catholics, the best means of leading to unity those who, with good faith, remain separated from it, accepting nothing but the gospel, but the whole gospel.

Thérèse soon deduced, with her intuition of the little way, that God's love for us, far from being opposed to his justice, is what allows him to conform us to it, on the sole condition that our faith frees us effectively and without reserve for this very love.

It was in September 1896 that Thérèse, in the course of a retreat, passed from her first intuition of the little way to that of her vocation to love alone, but a vocation in which all the possible demands of that love are included.

That apostolic element, which we have said was found already in the intentions of the first Teresa in reforming Carmel and which, similarly, is certainly found at least as

---

[12] Jn 15:5.

explicitly among the component parts of the vocation of
Thérèse, would at that time be defined and justified. Reading chapters 12 and 13 of the First Letter to the Corinthians, Thérèse, after having sought in vain for which of the
charisms in relation to the different ministries could really
be hers, passed to the conclusion, on charity (*agapē*). She
was seized by the conviction that what can, what must be
the proper vocation of the contemplative, especially the
Carmelite, in relation to the Church's apostolate is quite
simply to consecrate herself, to surrender herself without
reserve to this love, the end and, as it were, the soul of all
the particular charisms according to the Apostle. But, here
more than ever, we must leave the words to her:

> Finally, I had found rest. . . . Charity gave me the key to
> my vocation. I understood that, if the Church had a body,
> composed of various members, the most necessary, the
> most noble of all would not be lacking to it, I understood
> that the Church had a Heart, and that this Heart was burn-
> ing with Love. I understood that Love alone made all the
> members of the Church act, that if Love ever came to be
> extinguished, the Apostles would no longer proclaim the
> Gospel, the Martyrs would refuse to shed their blood. . . .
> I understood that Love comprised all vocations, that Love
> was all, that it embraced all times and all places. In a word,
> that it is eternal! . . .
>
> Then, in the excess of my delirious joy, I cried out: O
> Jesus, my Love . . . my vocation, finally I have found it, my
> vocation is love! . . .
>
> Yes, I have found my place in the Church, and it is you,
> O my God, who have given me this place. . . . In the Heart
> of the Church, my Mother, I shall be Love. . . . Thus I shall
> be everything. . . . Thus my dream will be realized![13]

[13] See Gaucher, *Histoire d'une vie*, 181ff.

But this discovery obviously presupposes a prior discovery of all that this "Love of God poured into our hearts by the Holy Spirit who has been given us", as Saint Paul himself says, is and implies and demands. And this discovery was effectively going to come out of the experience into which Thérèse would, as it were, plunge, during the final approach of her death: the disconcerting experience of dereliction, of faith torn by the sudden attack of endlessly renewed doubts. Faith would survive it only through the immensity of the love she recognized, made her own, with all the terrible demands of purity that its very fullness implied.

One last time, let us leave the words to her, so that she might lead us to the most mysterious aspect of her experience of union with Christ the Redeemer, up to the consummation of her own identification with sinners. Does Saint Paul again not say: "He who had not known sin [God] was made sin for us, so that in him we might become the justice of God" (2 Corinthians 5:21)?

Here, we must have recourse to the last conversations. Up until Easter 1896, she says to us:

> I enjoyed [at that time] a faith so lively, so clear that the thought of heaven made all my happiness, I couldn't believe that there were impious people without faith. I believed that they were speaking contrary to their real thoughts in denying the existence of heaven, of the beautiful heaven where God himself would like to be their eternal reward. In those very joyful days of Easter, Jesus made me feel that there truly are souls who do not have faith, who, through the abuse of grace, lose that precious treasure, the source of the only pure and true joys. He allowed my soul to be invaded by the thickest shadows and the thought of heaven, which was so sweet to me, to be no longer anything but a subject of combat and torment. . . . This trial was not to

last several days, several weeks, it was to be extinguished
only at the hour marked by the good God and . . . this hour
has not yet come. . . . I wish I could express what I mean,
but, alas! I believe it is impossible. One must have travelled
in this dark tunnel to understand the darkness of it.[14]

Now here is where the great paradox awaits us, and also
what can be considered, as it were, the summit of Thérèse's
testimony to our times: the preceding text, the one in which
Thérèse defines with such simplicity, such clarity the definitive awareness of her own vocation in the Mystical Body,
takes place at the same moment. This text in which she expresses her vocation to Love in all its demands: Love of God,
for God, without doubt, but first of all Love such as God
alone possesses it for all those he loves, beginning with the
worst sinners, Love that only the dereliction of Jesus on the
Cross can translate for us, express to us, make us enter into
that world of the Fall, this text, the vocation it describes,
takes place in just this period of exceptional trial!

Nothing, finally, could be more revealing, both of Thérèse,
of her most personal experience, and of the message with
which God invested her for our post-Christian world and
for this Church, which is herself not all that wonderful in
human eyes but which, nevertheless, has the responsibility
for carrying it to this world.

After what we have already said about the Thérèsian "little
way" as reflecting the true meaning of justification by faith,
and faith alone, what has just been added places in an undeniable light the total fallacy of the interpretation that Maxence van der Meersch[15] thought he could give of it, which
is, probably without even suspecting it, akin to the error in

---

[14] See Gaucher, *La Passion de Thérèse de Lisieux*, 56ff.

[15] I am thinking of the book by Maxence van der Meersch, *La Petite Sainte
Thérèse* (Paris, 1947).

which Luther was progressively immersed: as if God saved us without changing us, through a justice attributed purely as a result of our faith in the only just Jesus Christ. What Thérèse, in reality, understood so well and must make us understand is that God does not save us in virtue of some merit that we might attain by ourselves, even if with his help: completing, sustaining our own will but not creating it. Quite the contrary, Saint Paul himself, at the moment when he has just said to the Philippians: "Work for your salvation with fear and trembling" (an expression that means: with the greatest seriousness), nevertheless adds: "knowing that it is God who creates in you the will and the achievement".[16]

In other words, and to return to Thérèse, the little way, as a way of pure faith, is a way of total abandonment in the hands of God. For Christian faith is a faith in the love of God, persuaded not only that he has done everything *for us* in his crucified Son but that he will do everything *in us*: to the point of identifying us with the very Person of this Son, the Son of his love.

Which is to say that through this faith, still according to Saint Paul: "It is no longer I who live: it is Jesus who lives in me!": the supreme cry of Galatians 2:1!

If this is so, is it not necessary to come to the point of saying, in the final analysis, that the faith that saves, and par excellence that which not only saves us but contributes to the salvation of others, is a faith in which, just as it is no longer we who live, it is not even we who believe, but Christ who believes in us?

But, perhaps one will say, what meaning can that have? The same meaning that we have found in the affirmation of

[16] Phil 2:13.

Eckhart that the very possibility of *Abegescheidenheit*, the detachment necessary for *Gelazenheit*, the surrender to grace, itself depends on that *Gelazenheit*. More simply, the crucial experience, in all senses, for Thérèse is that, if faith is faith in divine Love, it is that Love itself that, taking charge even of our faith, ends in making it not only the faith that saves us but the faith that saves quite simply: cooperating in the salvation of which Christ alone nevertheless remains, in short, the sole author.

~

One can say that the link, or rather the first and unique source of all these aspects of Thérèse's testimony, which are so closely associated, is, under true inspiration from above, the return to the word of God, to the gospel centered in her heart (to repeat an expression by which she did not hesitate to extend Saint Paul himself). From this comes her principal rediscovery, for the Church of our times, that the entire gospel of Jesus (*evangelium Christi*) is the gospel of the Father. Let us listen to the gospel of the divine paternity, revealed in his unique Son made flesh, in order to make of all ourselves true children of God, as Saint John says. All the same, she could only rediscover it as she rediscovered it: by entering lucidly into "the Mystery" par excellence, the mystery of the divine "Kingdom", according to Saint Mark, the mystery of the Cross, explained by Saint Paul as the mystery of God and of us, reconciled, reunited in Christ, more precisely, in his body (and his soul!) on the Cross.

VI

ELIZABETH OF THE TRINITY

The Carmelite Vocation
and Life of Elizabeth Catez

There is so close a connection, first of all between Thérèse of Lisieux and Elizabeth of Dijon, then between those two and Edith Stein, that we bring our discussion of Thérèse to a conclusion only by gathering together in the end the sheaf of their three testimonies.

But, passing on to Elizabeth,[1] we must begin by stressing the close analogies between the destinies of these two French Carmelites, separated by less than a generation, but also the differences. Both came from a bourgeois, provincial family, but that of the Catez seems to have been more open to the contemporary world and a little more cultivated than that of the Martins. Above all, if Thérèse lost her mother at an early age, it was Elizabeth's father, a career officer, who died early. And, instead of coming as the last little one in a large family, the latter would have only one younger sister.

Elizabeth of the Trinity was canonized by Pope Francis on October 16, 2016. —ED.

[1] Everything that follows is based on the excellent critical edition, drawn up by Father Conrad de Meester, of all Elizabeth's writings: 3 volumes (Paris: Cerf, 1980). (The first of three volumes of the English translation was published by the Institute of Carmelite Studies in 1984, the other two volumes to follow.)

What is interesting in her situation is that her mother, a great reader of Teresa of Avila, communicated her enthusiasm to Elizabeth, but she took fright when she saw the Carmelite vocation emerge in her daughter and she resisted it for some time.

One factor whose importance has not perhaps been measured is the fact that the young Elizabeth had what one might call a worldly life, with parties and dances, receptions, and so forth, which were certainly innocent but included many encounters and friendships with other young people.[2] In particular, if her studies seem scarcely to have been carried much farther than those of Thérèse (in Carmel, both launched forth into numerous poems that had equally pious intentions but were just as consistently atrocious), Elizabeth showed an aptitude as well as a very lively taste for music. The one point on which her education surpasses, and by a great deal, that of Thérèse is this musical side. It seems indeed that this circumstance was not without influence not only over the direction of her whole orientation, which was certainly more contemplative than apostolic, but also over the importance that the theme of divine praise would assume for her.

There is without question a realistic, practical side to Thérèse, along with a sense and a taste for the concrete, including an excellent sense of humor, to which we will come back.

This is not at all the case with Elizabeth: Hans Urs von Balthasar has even stressed a tendency in her to a loftiness that is perhaps a bit too facile, and it would take the practice

[2] Otherwise it would be impossible to comprehend the number and variety of true letters of spiritual direction, but without a trace of pedantry, she would send from her monastery.

of a rigorous asceticism, and above all the intervention of a serious illness, to rid her of it.

The most obvious common external factor between the two Carmelites is that both, having entered Carmel at a very young age, were to die there, in great suffering, in a very short time.

On the other hand, if Thérèse entered a monastery that was, if not scandalous, in any case not one of the best, Elizabeth benefited from Prioresses and Novice Mistresses who were assuredly excellent religious and had, as well, remarkable personalities.[3]

Above all, at this Dijon Carmel where, soon with mixed feelings, her mother saw her visit, she would benefit, before even entering, from a retreat given by a Dominican, a serious theologian and a good spiritual guide: Father Vallée.[4] His influence over her should not be exaggerated, nor should only its good side be seen. Fairly eloquent, with a kind of eloquence very much of his times, he bore some of the responsibility for that cheap loftiness that she would have difficulty transcending and even more for a sentimental style that would undercut a few of her better texts.

One can nevertheless pardon him freely if one observes that he was certainly at the origin of the fundamentally doctrinal, and more precisely theological, character in the best sense of the words, of the overall spirituality that she would develop. In addition, the least one could say is that he

[3] I am thinking especially of Mother Marie of Jesus, the Prioress who accepted her at the Dijon Carmel and would later become the foundress of the Carmel at Paray-le-Monial, as well as of Mother Germaine, who would succeed her and would publish in 1909 a volume of reminiscences: *La Servante de Dieu Élisabeth de la Trinité*.

[4] Cf. Father de Meester's observation on p. 78 of the first volume of the *Oeuvres complètes* (English trans.: I:69–70).

certainly encouraged, if not awakened, Elizabeth's passionate interest in Holy Scripture (although obtained second-hand, as through Abbé Gaume's *Manuel*) and in particular in Saint Paul.

Born in 1880, having entered the Dijon Carmel in the month of August 1901, Elizabeth was to die in 1906, probably, according to the symptoms, from cancer of the stomach.

Elizabeth and Thérèse

There is no doubt that Elizabeth was acquainted with *Histoire d'une âme* and that it made a deep impression on her, indeed directly influenced her. I have already indicated, however, the clearly personal orientation that she was going to pursue in a very sustained way. Once again, with her, contemplation remained dominant. On the other hand, her acceptance of suffering was no less moving than that of her predecessor. But, in her case even more than in that of Thérèse, despite some ascetical practices, like the wearing of a hair-shirt, which she sometimes imposed on herself, it would be completely vain and positively absurd to suppose any kind of dolorism. Everything, in fact, seemed dominated, indeed absorbed, by the theme of divine praise.

But that invites us to pass from her formation to what seems to have been very early defined as her quite personal approach to the interior life.

To situate her in relation to Thérèse, it is unquestionably necessary to follow two themes that throw additional light on what she has in common with her, whether she received it from her or whether she got it from the same, principally biblical sources. The first of these themes, already mentioned, is that of praise, and more precisely, as she never ceased to insist: the praise of God's glory. The second is the very explicitly trinitarian character of the orientation of her prayer and of her whole existence, which could be described, in connection with the first theme, as eucharistic, in the most precise sense.

The constant presence of these two themes, either explicitly evoked or latent in the background of all she wrote, is certainly what constitutes her most personal note and what makes even texts that are not expressed in her best form easily recognizable as her own.

It could be said that they bring an enlargement and, as it were, a spiritual dilation to the Thérèsian themes of the vocation to love, of the little way, the way of spiritual childhood or, above all, total abandonment to suffering and death, even in darkness. This is not to say that their introduction necessarily presupposes a deepening. Thérèse, in one sense, remains incomparable through the simple heroism of her renunciation, her total self-forgetfulness. But each soul has her own vocation. If Elizabeth's end did not have the kind of tragic greatness as that of Thérèse, she had, she drew from it, a beauty that was both inexpressibly serene and touching.

I mean that there was, undeniably, in the dying Thérèse a sublime strength of soul despite her disarming simplicity. But, in the particularly delicate and sensitive being manifested by Elizabeth's letters and all we know of her, the serenity, the joy triumphing over atrocious suffering and also, what is perhaps not the least, over simple exhaustion, has indeed a beauty of its own that is perhaps not less admirable. Here, all effort at comparison is a bit ridiculous: there is nothing to choose between two vocations, two graces that complement each other.

But, again, it is appropriate, after this general glance, for us to quote and comment briefly on several particularly revealing texts.

It is obviously necessary to start with the theme of praise: praise of the divine glory, as she insists on it, as a good disciple of the Apostle. It is in fact this theme that would define for her what she herself felt to be her own vocation, such as love, or, as she says, the heart, was for Thérèse. It is true that she too seems to have grasped it only later in a fully conscious way. But, in doing this, both of them were only conceiving and formulating, after the event, in a very feminine way, what had captivated them early on, indeed right away. Elizabeth, for her part, was so attached to it that, indifferent to the barbarism, she would make *"laudem gloriae"* her own secret name (one can only think of the new name promised by the Apocalypse).

It is indicative of the importance that she attached to this theme that she treated it twice, in two parallel texts, written in the course of the same month of August 1906, which preceded her death by only three months. One is a spiritual letter-testament addressed to her younger (already married) sister, "Guite", as she called her familiarly. As for the second, it is her last personal retreat, in which one would say that she wanted to bring out explicitly for herself, at the end of her existence, what had as if completely magnetized her.

In this respect, the Carmelite Father Conrad de Meester, who has edited and provided a commentary for Elizabeth's texts,[5] duly emphasizes with what delicacy she adapts, here

[5] Ibid., 89ff. (English trans.: 87ff.).

for a tenderly and maternally loved sister, but in a similar way for many other friends, the fundamental theme par excellence of her monastic life. But how revealing it is that for her, with the necessary adaptations, she instinctively believes that the spirituality of a Christian laity living in the world should not differ in its essence from that of a strictly cloistered nun!

It might even be deemed significant that the first of these two texts, as Father de Meester has established, was the one addressed to her sister. There was therefore certainly, with Elizabeth as with Thérèse, an apostolic aspect, one of witness, that belonged to her vocation as a nun. The sole difference is that she did not have that special vocation of reaching, touching, moving decidedly toward the souls at the greatest distance from God. More simply, Elizabeth is a nun, if one might say so, certainly as much for others as for herself, but first of all quite simply, but not exclusively, for those close to her, family and friends. In fact, if Thérèse's influence can be rightly considered missionary, aimed especially at those outside the Church, Elizabeth's can be said rather to be inside the Church: aimed first of all to make Christians the most living members of Christ. Here, again, it seems that we are in the presence of two different but complementary vocations between which there is nothing to choose, nor is there, assuredly, any order of importance to be established.

Since what we are pursuing in this present volume is above all the actual or possible influence of these figures, which we have sought to grasp with a few particularly characteristic traits, we will concentrate on the text addressed to Guite rather than on the one that aspired, in addition to the edification of its author, only to a limited communication to her fellow sisters.

That will not prevent us from indicating in conclusion what in the "Dernière retraite" ["Last Retreat"] is characteristic with respect to fraternal instruction.

It is very remarkable that the text of this letter to Guite, like many others by Elizabeth, is full of quotations (or allusions), principally from Ruusbroec but also from Saint John of the Cross and, here, from Bossuet. In the present case, they center particularly on the theme, which we first noted in Hadewijch, of exemplarism, which Elizabeth very rightly connects with Pauline predestination in the sense that the Father from all eternity has seen and willed us in his Son. Precisely, she says, he has destined us to recognize his glory and to praise it, not only in our thoughts and words but through the offering of our whole life, of our whole being, which has become in Christ his own living image.

From this comes the conclusion toward which everything in this model for a retreat proposed to her sister as well as everything, again, in her entire religious life tended:

"We have been predestined by a decree of him who works all things according to the counsel of his will so that we may be the praise of his glory."

It is Saint Paul who speaks in this way, Saint Paul instructed by God himself. How are we to realize this great dream of our God's heart, this immutable will for our souls? How, in a word, are we to correspond to our vocation of becoming perfect praises of glory of the Most Holy Trinity? "In heaven each soul is a praise of glory to the Father, to the Word, to the Holy Spirit, because each soul is established in pure love" and "lives no longer its own life but the life of God". Then it knows him, Saint Paul says, as it is known by him, in other words "its understanding is the understanding of God, its will the will of God, its love the very love of God. It is in reality the Spirit of love

and strength that transforms the soul, for having been given
to it in order to supply what is lacking to him", as Saint
Paul again says, "he works in it this glorious transformation". Saint John of the Cross affirms that "The soul surrendered to love, through the power of the Holy Spirit, is
nearly raised to the degree of which we were just speaking"
already here below! That is what I call a perfect praise of
glory! A praise of glory is a soul who dwells in God, who
loves with a pure and disinterested love, without seeking
itself in the sweetness of this love; who loves him beyond
all his gifts and even if it has received nothing from him
and who desires the good for the object thus loved. Now
how can we effectively desire and will good to God if not
in accomplishing his will, since his will ordains everything
for his greater glory? Thus this soul must surrender itself
fully, madly, to the point of willing nothing but what God
wills.[6]

Supported by this fabric of quotations from Ruusbroec,
Saint John of the Cross, but above all from Saint Paul, she
would now launch into the development that follows, which
is wholly personal (and how revealing of what is most personal to her!):

A praise of glory is a soul of silence who holds herself like a
lyre beneath the mysterious touch of the Holy Spirit so that
he can draw divine harmonies from it; she knows that suffering is a chord that produces still more beautiful sounds,
so she loves to see it on her instrument so as to move the
heart of her God more delightfully.

A praise of glory is a soul that gazes on God in faith and
simplicity; it is a reflector of all that he is; it is, as it were, a

[6] Father de Meester has pointed out, in parentheses, the references to the
Spiritual Canticle and the *Living Flame* of Saint John of the Cross, and, in
footnotes, the ones to Ruusbroec, whom she had just read with enthusiasm
(ibid., 123f. [English trans.: 119]).

bottomless abyss over which he can flow out, pour out; it is also like a crystal through which he can radiate and contemplate all his perfections and his own splendor. A soul who thus allows the divine Being to satisfy in her his need to communicate "all that he is and all that he has" is in reality the praise of glory of all his gifts.

Finally, a praise of glory is a being who is always giving thanks. Each of her actions, her movements, each of her thoughts, her aspirations, at the same time that they are rooting her more deeply in love, are like an echo of the eternal Sanctus.

In the heaven of glory, the blessed "have no rest neither day nor night, saying: Holy, holy, holy, the Lord God Almighty. . . . And falling down, they adore him who lives forever. . . ."

In the heaven of her soul, the praise begins already her work of eternity. Her song is interrupted, for she is under the action of the Holy Spirit, who effects everything in her, and, although she is not always aware of it, for the weakness of nature does not allow her to be established in God without distractions, she sings always, she adores always, she has, so to speak, passed into praise and love, into the passion of the glory of her God. In the heaven of our soul, let us be praises of glory of the Holy Trinity, praises of love of our Immaculate Mother. One day the veil will fall, we will be introduced into the eternal courts, and there we will sing in the bosom of infinite Love. And God will give us "the new name promised to the victor". What will it be? . . .

LAUDEM GLORIAE![7]

Perhaps one will grumble a bit at this mention of God delighting particularly in a praise that goes up from suffering? Let us admit that there is, at least verbally, some trace

[7] Ibid., at the foot of the page.

in this of the dolorist language of the period: and yet there is indeed a proof of a love responding to love given by the one who persists, unshaken, to express himself, to stand fast, even though he draws no reward for himself!

Rather, instead of wasting our time with this pointless quibbling, let us note the insistence, first of all, on the paradox of the silent soul who, properly, since it is silent, can vibrate beneath the finger of God to his pure praise. Thus this simplicity, this self-forgetfulness that allows us to be absorbed in him to the point of reflecting him. Finally, as a result, the absorption of all existence in thanksgiving: let us understand, as Elizabeth obviously does, a praise that implies sacrifice to God of everything he has given us, rendering him love for love, a love like his own, since, even in our own hearts, it is still his own that has made ours. After that, one understands how she might say that such a life is, as it were, an inauguration of eternal life here on earth, the only difference being that it is now through faith, in faith, that we live what will be the very object of the beatific vision.

Once this fundamental theme has been identified, it is easy to see how the acceptance of suffering and death is integrated into it, a theme discreetly evoked even in the retreat plan drafted for her sister but which, in her last retreat for herself, would be extensively developed.

This is precisely where we should expect her to spell out in what sense she understands this acceptance. This expectation will not be disappointed.

First of all, as Father de Meester emphasizes, this acceptance must be read in the perspective of identification with Christ himself. As a letter written at the same time as the retreat in question says:

I so wish that the Father could recognize in me the image of the One crucified by love!

And another:

This is what I am going to teach myself: conformity, identity with my adored Master, the One crucified by love. Then I shall be able to fulfill my office of praise of glory.[8]

In other words, what attracts her is not the suffering; it is, as she will say: "Love hidden in the Cross".[9]

The clarification given this by the last retreat leaves nothing more to be desired:

"Strip off the old man in whom you lived your previous life, [God] tells me, and clothe yourself with the new man who was created according to God, in justice and holiness." This is the path marked out, it is only a matter of stripping ourselves in order to follow it as God wills! To strip ourselves, to die to self, to lose sight of ourselves, it seems to me that this is what the Master had in mind when he said: "If anyone wishes to come after me, let him take up his cross and renounce himself." "If you live according to the flesh", the Apostle also says, "you will die; but if you put to death in the Spirit the works of the flesh, you will live." This is the death God asks for and of which he says: "Death has been swallowed up in victory." "O death", says the Lord, "I will be your death": which is to say, O soul, my adopted daughter, look at me and you will lose sight of yourself; flow entirely into my Being, come die in me so that I might live in you![10]

Nothing could be more clear. But again we must quote the marvelous development that she will give to these final words:

---

[8] Quoted on 149 (English trans.: 135).

[9] Ibid.

[10] Ibid., 173–74 (English trans.: 152).

"Be perfect as your heavenly Father is perfect." When my Master makes me understand these words in the depths of my soul, it seems to me that he is asking me to live like the Father "in an eternal present", "with no before, with no after", but entirely in the unity of my being in this "eternal now". What is this present? Here it is David who answers me: "He will always be adored because of himself."

That is the eternal present in which *Laudem gloriae* must be established. But in order for her to be true in this attitude of adoration, for her to be able to sing: "I awake the dawn", she must also be able to say with Saint Paul: "For the sake of his love, I have lost everything"; that is: because of him, in order to adore him always, I am "isolated from, separated from, stripped of" myself and all things, with regard to both the natural and the supernatural gifts of God. For a soul who is not thus "destroyed and freed" from itself will of necessity be trivial and natural at certain times, and this is not worthy of a daughter of God, of a bride of Christ, of a temple of the Holy Spirit. To guard against this natural life, the soul must be wholly vigilant in her faith, with her gaze turned toward the Master. Then she "will walk" as the king and prophet says, "in the integrity of her heart within her house". Then she "will always adore her God because of himself" and will live in this eternal present where he lives.[11]

Let us note: according to the testimony of all who knew her as well as according to everything she left us, nothing is perhaps more striking in this very sweet young person of so fragile a tenderness than her complete detachment from self. But such a detachment is possible only if one lives no longer in oneself but in Another. That leads us finally to the text by Elizabeth that is undoubtedly the most often reproduced and whose very substance is, as it were, given in

[11] Ibid., 174 (English trans.: 152–53).

a single phrase in the last paragraph of the text we have just read: her prayer to the Trinity, in which she envisages the personal relations with each of the three Persons implied by the life of grace in us as an association with that life of love that is the life of God, One and Three.

Our Life in the Trinity

This text, so widespread and commented upon so extensively, is nevertheless not without weaknesses. Its extreme density results in an abstraction that would give an impression of dryness if nothing corrected it. It seems that Elizabeth foresaw this. Unfortunately, what she did to prevent it: a few touches of calculated pathos (obviously in the style of Father Vallée), is testimony to the trouble she had in ridding herself of these ornaments that are more annoying than edifying. The importance of the themes treated accentuates these weaknesses, which cannot, however, succeed in eclipsing it.

> O my God, Trinity whom I adore, help me to forget myself entirely so that I may be established in you, still and peaceful, as if my soul were already in eternity. May nothing trouble my peace or make me leave you, O my Immutable One, but let each minute carry me farther into the depths of your Mystery. Give peace to my soul, make it your heaven, your beloved dwelling and the place of your repose. May I never leave you there alone, but may I be wholly present, wholly vigilant in my faith, wholly adoring, wholly surrendered to your creative action.
>
> O my beloved Christ, crucified by love, I wish to be a bride for your Heart, I wish to cover you with glory, I wish to love you . . . until I die of it! But I feel my weakness, and I ask you to "clothe me with yourself", to identify my soul

with all the movements of your soul, to overwhelm me, invade me, substitute yourself for me so that my life might be but a radiance of your Life. Come into me as Adorer, as Restorer, as Savior. O Eternal Word, Word of my God, I want to spend my life listening to you, I want to make myself wholly teachable so as to learn everything from you. Then, through all the nights, all the voids, all the weakness, I want to gaze on you always and remain beneath your great light; O my beloved Star, fascinate me so that I might no longer leave your radiance.

O consuming Fire, Spirit of love, "come upon me", so that an incarnation of the Word, so to speak, might take place in me: that I might be another humanity for him in which he renews his whole Mystery. And you, O Father, bend over your poor little creature, "cover her with your shadow", see in her only the "Beloved in whom you are well pleased".

O my Three, my All, my Beatitude, infinite Solitude, Immensity in which I lose myself, I surrender myself to you like a victim. Bury yourself in me so that I might bury myself in you, while waiting to go contemplate the abyss of your greatness in your light.

November 21, 1904[12]

The date *in fine* is enough to indicate that this text is prior to that full maturity that Elizabeth seems to have reached only in her final months, when suffering had, as it were, weaned her from all affectation. We know that she was familiar with the work of Msgr. Gay, that modest popularizer of the last century, from what Bremond baptized "the French school". Needless to say, we suspect here a little of that mimicry that is a common weakness of the most youthful, great feminine admiration: something with the scent of

[12] Ibid., 200–201 (English trans.: 183–84). Father de Meester's commentary is found on pages 126ff. of vol. II.

chocolate candy seems to have passed from the Bishop of
Anthédon and his Bérullism to honey water in the still too
candid disciple!

Despite even this, all the themes are there and very much
in place. The life of the Trinity in us is well described as
being, rather, our life absorbed in it. The whole is a matter of the increasingly conscious presence of the soul, of
the whole human being, in that peace of the divine depths:
plunged into what makes, as Eckhart said more prosaically,
the interior "*bullitio*" of the divine life manifest itself by
prolonging itself in the "*ebullitio*" of creation.

It is Christ, and Christ crucified as the bearer of divine
Love to creatures sunk deep in their sin, who, having accomplished this divine work for us, will accomplish it in us by
accomplishing himself, as Saint Paul says to the Ephesians,
in those souls he espouses in a totally surrendered faith. Invaded by this perfect Adorer of the Father made man with
our fallen humanity, Atoner of his offense, Savior of his
decay, the voice of the eternal Word, of the Word of God
who has become one of them, teaches them then how to
achieve his plan for them, thus plunging them into what, in
the eyes of their weakness, is darkness but in the end will
reveal itself, to their faith fascinated by such a Love, to be,
as it were, the inaccessible light in which God dwells.

Then, too, conjointly, inseparably, this fire of the Spirit
will seem to consume them only in order to consummate
their union, their identification with the humanity of the
Word, with the Mystery of the Cross ending in the Mystery of "the two-in-one flesh": that Shadow of God who
had covered the virginity of Mary, covering them in their
turn, will let nothing but that "Beloved in whom he is well
pleased" be seen in them in the very eyes of the invisible

Father. And God will lose us in Him as he willed to be lost in us.

These seeming attempts at explanation are only a sketch of one of innumerable ways in which what she meant could be expressed but which no one will ever manage to express in a satisfactory fashion. The sole merit of these attempts, if there be one, might well be to show that such a vision of faith, on the whole, transcends us to such a degree that Elizabeth's own manner, precisely because it is more naïve, can bring out far more of the inexpressible than we can touch here. . . .

~

As was the case with Thérèse, so for Elizabeth, for both together, it is in finishing our journey, in considering Edith Stein, that it will be possible for us to suggest a few conclusions that are perhaps not completely inconclusive.

VII

EDITH STEIN

Edith Stein's Position

Edith Stein, whom the present Pope [John Paul II] recently beatified (as he did Elizabeth of the Trinity): Blessed Teresa Benedicta of the Cross, as it is thus fitting now to invoke her, shares with many converts, beginning with Newman, the fact of being as little and as poorly understood with respect to where she ended up as to where she began. How many Jews, at least among those who claim to be representatives of their people, were not indignant about this beatification and seemed completely unaware of the fact that it was out of fidelity to this people from which she was born that this Catholic Christian accepted death! But the Catholics, on their side, especially, too, some of those who professed particularly to be representatives of their Faith, seemed not to know what to do with this baptized person who remains an intruder for them. As welcome as was the opinion of Jacques Maritain, saying that her work merited being translated into French and made better known, how revealing were his reservations: "Despite", he said, "her rather unorthodox Thomism". . . . Why should the only orthodox Thomism be, apparently, that which admits of no other interpretation but that of John of Saint Thomas, as distant as that is from the proper conception that Thomas himself had

Teresa Benedicta of the Cross was canonized by Pope John Paul II on October 11, 1998.—ED.

of both philosophy as well as theology and their relationship? It is one of those mysteries we will not try to clear up!

In fact, despite such hostilities and hesitations, both the
work and the personality of this so poorly loved "Blessed"
could very well one day appear as having shown the decisive way toward reconciliation between Judaism and the
Church. It could equally be true that she has shown to Christians themselves a renewed approach to their spiritual tradition that makes it attractive to their contemporaries by re-
animating it on their own behalf.

Born in Breslau, in Silesia,[1] in a Jewish family, in 1891,
Edith Stein was to lose her father almost immediately. But
her mother, profoundly religious, took up the management
of the lumber business that insured the living of the family, without ceasing, however, to watch over the upbringing
of her eleven children, seven of whom would reach adult
age. While retaining, it seems, a high moral sense, but not
her mother's fidelity to Jewish beliefs and practices, Edith,
for her part, manifested very early not only an exceptional

---

[1] The Prioress of the Cologne Carmel, Mother Maria Amata Neyer has
written a short biography, *La Bienheureuse Edith Stein: Soeur Thérèse-Bénédicte
de la Croix*, trans. into French by Conrad de Meester (Paris: Cerf, 1987).

We have, unfortunately, only mediocre French translations of *Finite and
Eternal Being* (Louvain-Paris, 1972) and *The Science of the Cross* (ibid., 1957),
whose translators did not even conscientiously correct the proofs. The texts
translated with commentaries by Philibert Secrétan (*Phénoménologie et Philosophie chrétienne* [Paris, 1987]) were not handled as badly but are far from presenting the desirable accuracy.

The *Complete Works of Edith Stein* are in the process of being translated
into English and published by the Institute of Carmelite Studies in Washington, D.C. *The Science of the Cross* is available in an earlier English translation
(Chicago: Henry Regnery, 1960).

I profited much from the book by J. M. Oesterreicher (himself a convert
from German Judaism, later a priest in the United States): *Walls Are Crumbling*
(New York: Devin, 1952), not only from his chapter on Edith Stein but also
from those on Husserl and especially on Adolf Reinach.

intelligence but also a very strong personality. Dissatisfied with her secondary studies, she interrupted them to spend a year in Hamburg, at the home of her older sister, who was expecting her second baby and did not get along well with her husband. Having, it seems, helped to straighten out the situation, Edith returned to Breslau the following year and prepared to finish her interrupted studies. In 1911, her examination for the *Abitur* would be a great success.

She had in the meantime lost all faith but not all religious preoccupation. Enrolled immediately at the University of Breslau, she flitted from one course to another, at first following psychology. But she heard about the phenomenology that Edmund Husserl had begun to develop at Göttingen, and she went there the following year.

There is no doubt that this new orientation took on a decisive importance right away not only for her thinking but also for her life. Husserl, in those days, exercised an unexpected influence, besides, over a whole circle of students and collaborators.[2]

His insistence, inspired by his mentor Brentano, who was himself very well-informed about medieval philosophy, on the primordial importance of the relation of thought to its object would very often have for them effects that completely transcended it. While he himself, despite this point of departure, came back to or rather put his trust in the radical subjectivism that characterized up to that point all post-Kantian thought, many of his disciples would receive from it the impetus that would free them from it and, at the same stroke, many times lead them to a religious conversion.

Such was the case with Adolf Reinach, another Jew who had broken off from his ancestral faith, in whom Husserl

---

[2] Cf. Oesterreicher, 49ff. and 99ff. in particular.

found a disciple and collaborator of such quality that he came
to say, not without a sense of humor that made him singularly attractive, that he himself did not understand in depth
his own *Logische Untersuchungen* until Reinach had given his
commentary on them![3]

It was this Reinach who welcomed Edith to Göttingen,
and the impression made on her by this welcome was equally
revealing to her of his personality: always open to others
and generous in sharing his riches, but not without a touch
of maternal authoritarianism that she sometimes set about to
overcome; from this first encounter with Reinach, she was
struck by his smiling attention to the other, by his openness
in which there was nothing dominating or possessive.[4]

This "empathy", which is the principle of all Husserl's
phenomenological research, which is to say, not only a sympathy necessary to an authentic understanding of what one
is studying but an effort to place oneself literally within the
object studied, would be the theme of Edith's doctoral dissertation. But Husserl, for his part, could not be long is dis-
cerning the exceptional quality of his new student. When
the 1914 war occurred, Edith interrupted her studies again
to serve with the Red Cross.

When it ended, in 1916, and with her thesis brilliantly
defended, as we can well believe, Husserl, who had just accepted a chair at Freiburg im Breisgau, asked her to accompany him as his assistant.

The collaboration between the two was not to be without shadows. Edith deplored the fact that he himself did
not develop all the possibilities that she was not alone in
perceiving in his method and which were used by him only

---

[3] Ibid., 79ff.
[4] Ibid., 332.

for modifications in earlier works, while he began, for his part, to lock himself into the at least apparent subjectivism *redivivus* of the *Ideen* and then the *Cartesian Meditations*.

He would nonetheless have the kindness and also the generosity to send her the most flattering recommendation, anticipating that she would eventually obtain a lecture chair (an unheard of thing for a woman in that period). In fact, such a hope was premature, never to be realized.

Yet, in the meantime, Reinach, mobilized to the front, had come to the Christian Faith, as had his wife, Anne. Both had been baptized in a Protestant church. But he himself did not hide his attraction toward the Catholic Church. He was killed the following year, not having been able to achieve what was for him no more than a vague anticipation. His wife, however, and nearly all his family would soon follow that path to the end.[5]

Edith, who collaborated with his wife in preparing an edition of a work he had left in progress (a philosophy of religion),[6] was struck by the fact that this faith, which was so recent, transfigured the despair of the young wife into a proof of true spiritual rebirth.

At the same time, it seems likely, despite her extreme reserve on this subject, that she was led to reject a hope of marriage that she had entertained until then.[7]

But a providential accident triggered a revelation that she must have been seeking at that time. In 1921, she paid a visit to the home of her friends Hedwig and Conrad Martius, whom she had known at Göttingen: both enthusiastic about philosophical research, they had withdrawn to a vast estate at Bergzabern in the Rheinpfalz, where they lived off

[5] Ibid., 133–34.
[6] Ibid., 135.
[7] See Mother Maria Amata, 33.

the produce from an orchard and received guests desiring to
share some time in their meditative retreat. One day when
she had remained there alone, Edith picked up in the library
a translation of the *Life of Saint Teresa of Avila*. Fascinated,
she could not put it down until the following morning. The
Christian Faith and more than the outline of a religious vocation were definitively imprinted on her with this reading.[8]

The same day, she went to town to buy a catechism and a
missal, soon followed by a breviary. Before even being baptized, she attended daily Mass at the church in Bergzabern.
But, very concerned to help her mother understand (the
latter had at first been terror-stricken by this conversion)
that this was not a denial of her Judaism but a renewal and
a fulfillment, she would accompany her to services at the
synagogue every time she passed through Breslau again, following the Psalms of the synagogal office in her breviary.[9]

Baptized on January 1, 1922, at Bergzabern, she was confirmed on February 2 by the Bishop of Spire, Msgr. Sebas-
tian, in his own chapel. She could not, on the other hand,
despite the recommendation of Husserl, obtain a university
assignment. But the Vicar General, Joseph Schwindt, soon
placed her in contact with the Dominicans of the city, and
the latter received her at their convent of Sainte-Madeleine
to teach at their school for young girls and at the institute
of formation for Catholic instructors, both of which were
under their supervision.

Dietrich von Hildebrand, at that time a disciple of Husserl,
had, for his part, put her in touch with the Jesuit Erich Przywara,[10] who would guide her, as he alone could, in the ac-

---

[8] Ibid., 34.

[9] Cf. Oesterreicher, 345.

[10] This very great spirit was exactly what she needed in order to enter into
the Catholic Faith, bringing with her what she had received from the best of
philosophy as of Judaism.

quisition of an excellent Catholic education. He began by having her translate into German the journals and letters of Newman, before leading her into a translation with commentary of Thomas Aquinas' *De Veritate*.

He then introduced her to the Benedictine Abbey of Beuron and its Abbot at the time, Dom Raphael Walzer.[11] Joseph Schwindt, who had been her spiritual adviser until his death in 1927, was succeeded in this responsibility by the Abbot. From then on, Edith led a nearly monastic life, teaching at Spire or stopping for prolonged retreats, very near the monastery, in the "House of the wooden bridge".

She does not hide from us the fact that, in the enthusiasm of her conversion, she would have, by herself, been brought to live only for heaven, turning aside from all earthly occupations, including those of the intellect. Her introduction by Przywara to Newman and Thomas together made her understand the romanticism of this attitude. In fact, in the years that followed, she combined her teaching with a true apostolate of conferences, for she was invited to them from all sides by Catholic intellectual circles, in the full excitement of renewal in Catholic Germany in the 1930s.

Over and above contributions like the study she gave in 1929 to a volume of collected essays offered to Husserl for his seventieth birthday: *The Phenomenology of Husserl and the Philosophy of Saint Thomas*, her translation with commentary of *De Veritate* brought her both intellectual and spiritual orientation.[12] It will be remembered that we began by studying the fundamental place of Christian exemplarism in the spirituality of Hadewijch of Antwerp. At the very moment when Hadewijch was living and writing, for her part, without even

[11] Having myself known Dom Walzer, who was one of those who introduced me to Catholicism, I have no trouble understanding well what Edith Stein must have owed to him.

[12] *Des hl. Thomas von Aquino Untersuchungen über die Wahrheit* (Breslau, 1931).

suspecting the existence of the Dominican master, Saint
Thomas had finished a brilliant renewal of this theme. Edith,
in turn, took it during these years as the point of departure
for a fundamental organization of the spiritual perspective
that would remain her own.

One could say that she found in this work both the transcendence and the integration of metaphysical realism and
idealism between which Husserl seemed to remain hesitant.
Confirmed by Saint Thomas in the assurance that her first
true master had given her: that all human thought and activity can only be suspended in the fully lived and consciously
realized relationship of our limited being with a transcendent Object, she now discovered, in the school of *De Veritate*, that, on the other hand, it is only by being absorbed in
the eternal thought that God has of us in his Son from all
eternity that we can hope to become truly ourselves: to realize the plan, the divine vocation that alone can give meaning, his meaning to human life.[13]

In a parallel way, Beuron would offer her an introduction to the fullness of the liturgical life of the Church, clarified by the instructions of Dom Walzer. She found there
the certitude that this divine vocation asks that we enter,
with all our soul and our entire being, into this revelation
that is made to us by the Word, the living Word of God
made flesh. The sacramental celebration places this revela-

---

[13] It is this study in particular that explains the animosity of so many Neo-
Thomists with regard to Edith Stein. It is not that she could be accused of
having misinterpreted *De Veritate*, it is much rather the attention she devoted
to it that is its cause! Typical is the hostility frankly acknowledged by Father
Sertillanges for this work: as if this were a disgraceful defect in Thomas,
altering the purity of his philosophy, that had completed Aristotle by Plato
in order to reunite a wholly biblical view of the presence of his created work
from all eternity in the thought and love of God! One finds in Oesterreicher,
on the other hand, (340ff.) a very sympathetic commentary on Edith's work.

tion within our reach in the holy Liturgy, and, if we surrender ourselves to it with faith, our entire life is refashioned according to the eternal plan of God. That already meant for her that to accept the designs of God over us, discovered in Christ, is of necessity to accept the Cross. But the holy weeks spent at Beuron were to convince her equally that the Cross thus recognized and effectively accepted, in communion with Christ dead and glorified, is, already now in the present, an anticipation of the resurrection, of eternal life, not only with God but in God.

This is what is explained in her wonderful essay on "The Prayer of the Church".[14]

The whole object of it, passing beyond all the fallacious distinctions and oppositions that were then dividing the different spiritual schools in Catholicism, and which have not ceased to do so, is to show, with as much strength as simplicity, how the prayer of the Church is that liturgical prayer of which the Mass, the eucharistic celebration of the Mystery of the Faith, which is itself the Cross, is the heart and which the prayer of all times first prepares and extends. But, in the prolongation, in the spirit of the latter, all individual prayer, all prayer of a believer fully conscious of all these riches of his Faith, becomes and consumes this prayer of the Church by assimilating us personally to the whole plan of God for each of us, in all the details of existence.

The same years when she was developing on her own behalf and beginning to translate for her contemporaries this progressive realization at which she had arrived: of the

[14] This study has been translated into French, in 1955, in the Éditions de Orante: *La Prière de l'Église*, but seems to have been overlooked by the French public. For an English translation see "The Prayer of the Church" in *The Collected Works of Edith Stein*, v. 4, *The Hidden Life*, trans. Waltraut Stein (Washington, D.C.: ICS Publications, 1992), 7–17.

Christian Mystery as the mystery of God that is alone able
to illuminate and achieve the mystery of man, Edith was
drawing the consequences of it for the proper vocation of
women. In conjunction with the development of her task as
educator, and particularly as educator of educators who were
themselves devoted particularly to the education of women,
she very soon took an interest in the problem of the eman-
cipation of women in the modern world. From there, she
had in turn come to rethink completely that problem itself
from within her discovery and acceptance of the Mystery
that Saint Paul designates as the mystery of "Christ in us,
our hope of glory". This, in turn, was the subject of a series
of essays, the most notable and advanced of which considers what she calls "The Ethos of Women's Vocations". [15]
But we will keep this text for the general conclusion of this
book, for which it will provide the foundation.

It is time, before that, to go on to the passion that will in
a way be the test and the occasion for the supreme achievement of a thought and an experience that can both be described as mystical, in the true and fundamental sense of
the expression: that is to say, perceived, conceived, not only
from the perspective but, as it were, from within the accomplishment in herself of the Mystery of the Cross of Jesus,
the Word of God made flesh.

The Achievement of Edith Stein

While Edith was in the process of coming to Christianity,
where she had from the start the assurance not only of find-
ing once again but precisely of fulfilling, in the most radical

[15] *Das Ethos der Frauenberufe* (Augsburg, 1931).

sense of the expression, her Judaism, events were moving quickly in Germany.

Nazism had taken power, and it was increasingly clear that the eradication of Judaism, which was one of its immediate objectives, had every chance of preceding and preparing the way for a no less, and perhaps even more, inexorable assault against Christian faith and existence.

In 1932, Heidegger, that wonder child (and prodigal son) of Husserl, apparently lost on "roads that lead nowhere" of an existentialism inspired as if by a fascination with nothingness, having become rector of the University of Fribourg, had shut his mentor out of it.[16]

Edith had finally at that time just obtained a university position, at the Catholic Pedagogical Institute, attached to the University of Münster. But, the following year, she was similarly fired.

On October 14 of the same year, she entered the Carmel of Cologne.[17]

With that team spirit that is the affliction of the best religious orders, a Carmelite who justifiably admires Edith has managed to see in this joining of the Carmelite tradition an abandonment, on Edith's part, of what Beuron had transmitted to her and, in particular, of its exaltation of liturgical prayer as the source of the whole prayer of the Church.

This interpretation makes no sense. What we have summarized of her little treatise on this theme has sufficiently shown that, for Edith, there was no opposition between liturgical prayer and personal prayer: it was liturgical prayer

[16] The latter took nothing away from the power of Heidegger's thought but warned of the uncertainty in which its own author seemed to have remained for a while about the final meaning that was to emerge from it.

[17] See the details in Mother Maria Amata, 61ff.

itself that convinced her that it should be extended and, in a way, blossom into the most personal of all Christian prayer to the point where it would invade and permeate her whole existence.

In consecrating herself in the present circumstances to the monastic life in its Carmelite form, she who would take then the characteristic name of Sister Teresa Benedicta of the Cross was entering at the same time both the order illuminated by the prophetic vocation of Elijah—who fled all idols into the solitude in which the people of God of the Old Covenant had carried out its initial exodus—and also the perspective of Teresa of Avila as explained and pushed to its farthest limits by John of the Cross.

In other words, in Edith's Carmelite vocation, it is necessary to recognize the urgent need she experienced, in the tragic circumstances in which she saw herself placed along with the people who had ceased to be her own, to consent freely to the Cross with which this people had once burdened Christ and who now, how mysteriously, were going to be as if identified entirely with him.

Once again, her first movement, entering the monastery as if it were the Via Crucis, was to abandon all her intellectual work for the exclusive, direct search for God, which the Benedictine Rule is the first to make the entire meaning of monastic life, no matter in what color habit it be pursued. But this time it was her own superiors who, after she had made her year's novitiate, stipulated that, quite on the contrary, she was to finish the large work that she had begun before she entered.

Completed in 1936, this work, outlined as early as 1931, explains how the philosophical search for truth can only end in the discovery of the living God and our abandonment in faith to the grace of filiation in view of which, according to eternal divine predestination, we were created in time.

Immediately delivered for typesetting, this book, devoted to *Endliches und Ewiges Sein* [*Finite and eternal being*],[18] could not be printed because of Hitler's anti-Semitic laws. It would appear only after the war, in 1950.

Two years later, the worsening of measures of this kind led the superiors to transfer to the Carmel of Echt, in the Netherlands, both Edith and her sister Rosa, who had also in turn converted and rejoined her at the monastery.

Edith undertook there her final work, which she would leave unfinished: *The Science of the Cross*.[19] One might say that it is like a *retractatio*, in the sense given the term by Saint Augustine, of John of the Cross' theology of the mystical experience, clarified by the phenomenology of the created spirit and the uncreated spirit, which the preceding treatise had outlined. . . .

She had intentionally undertaken it as a direct preparation for the precisely crucial trial in which the Jewish people were engaged from that time on and in which she had a presentiment that she too would be called, in one way or another, to take her part. . . .

On August 2, 1942, in a reprisal for a protest made by the Dutch Bishops against the persecution of the Jews, all the Jewish Catholics in the country were in turn arrested. Taken to Auschwitz with her sister, Edith was executed there with her on August 9, along with her Jewish brothers and sisters.

---

[18] See note 1 concerning the French translation, which was less scandalous than that of *The Science of the Cross* but very deficient nonetheless.

[19] See note 1.

"Ultima Verba"

As we have done in our preceding chapters, we will end this one with a quotation from several texts that are most particularly expressive of Edith Stein's message. But, while up to now we have accompanied the quotations with commentaries intended to help the reader of today in grasping the permanent timeliness of these quotations, we will let her speak alone: there is no better contemporary commentary on the continuity of the tradition that we have tried to bring out than that of Blessed Teresa Benedicta of the Cross, whose very choice of name is so significant.

We will begin with a series of texts drawn from *Finite and Eternal Being*, which one could call the discontinued continuity from the Trinity to the Incarnation. Next and finally, *The Science of the Cross* will show us how this continuity, which is that of this Love not only that God has but that God is, is pursued and made perfect in the redemptive Incarnation and our union with Christ as a union with his glorifying Cross.

Here, first of all, on the Trinity:

> Beside the manifestation of the divine name "I am", one finds in the Old Testament this formula with respect to creation: "Let us make man in our image", which our theologians interpret as a first sign of the mystery of the Trinity; it is also fitting to note the words of the Savior: "My Father and I are one." The "we", insofar as a unity constituted by the I and the thou, is a unity superior to that formed by the I. It is, in its most perfect sense, a unity of love. Love, insofar as adherence to a good, can be understood as love of self, but love is more than such an adherence, such an appreciation of value. It is a gift of self to a

thou, and, in its perfection, it gives birth to a unique being. Since God is love, the divine being must be the unique being of a plurality of Persons and his "I am" is tantamount to a "I give myself entirely to a thou", or "I am but one with a thou and thus we are one".

. . . The interior life of God is the entirely free, immutable and eternal reciprocal love of the Divine Persons between themselves. Their reciprocal gift is the unique, eternal, infinite existential essence that perfectly embraces each of them and all together. The Father offers it, from all eternity, to the Son by engendering him, and, while the Father and the Son give themselves to each other, the Holy Spirit proceeds from them. He is their reciprocal love and their gift. . . . [It is a question] of a perpetual production of self coming from the depths of infinite being as such: it is a question of a gift offered by the eternal I to the eternal Thou, of an eternal reception of self and of an always new gift of self. And, since the unique being eternally springs forth in this gift and this reception, because it commonly produces from it what is given and what is received, since the unique being is necessarily fruitful, the circle of God's inner life closes in consequence in the Third Person, who is gift, love and life.[20]

And now here is the text on the eternal Word and creation:

[There is something like] a double fact of the Logos, insofar as he is both the divine essence (the image of the Father) and the archetype, the first cause of all created things. Since the plan of creation, like all that exists in God, is eternal, the Logos and creation coincide from all eternity, although creation had a beginning in time and is subject to a development. In engendering the Son, in pronouncing the

---

[20] *Finite and Eternal Being*, p. 351 of the French trans.

Word, the Father restores to him the creation that he has foreseen from all eternity.[21]

And, to end, here is the meaning of the Cross:

The sufferings of the Dark Night are a participation in the Passion of Christ, and especially in his deepest suffering: God's abandonment. This consideration is confirmed expressly by the *Spiritual Canticle*, since there the ardent desire for the hidden God seems to be, as it were, the torment that dominates the whole mystical way. It does not even cease in the bliss of the bridal union. It adds to it, in a certain sense, through the growing knowledge that the soul receives there of God and of his love. Thanks to this knowledge, the presentiment of what will bring us the clear vision of God in glory increases in intensity. . . . During the whole of his life, Christ was unceasingly in possession of the Beatific Vision, up to the time of his agony in the Garden of Olives. Then, by an act of his free will, this delight was withdrawn from him. What human suffering, even if provoked by the most burning desire, could be compared with the torment that the Man-God must have experienced? Just as the human heart and spirit are powerless to conceive and taste the eternal beatitude, so they are incapable of perceiving the unfathomable mystery of such a privation. Only he who has experienced it can give something of it to taste. He does this to those he has chosen in the intimacy of the bridal union in order to share his sufferings. . . .[22]

[21] Ibid., 353.
[22] *The Science of the Cross*, 194.

CONCLUSION

We have written this whole book to show what essential contribution women have made, as they alone could do, first of all in the Church of the Middle Ages, which was beginning to decline, then in that of the Renaissance and Reformation, when the decline had become such that a return to nature signified a new paganism and a return to grace, schism and heresy.

Finally, in the anemic Church of the post-Christian world, here are three of them at once who lead us back to the purest sources of the gospel, Saint Paul and the great liturgical tradition of the beginnings, in words and with a manner that appeal just as much to the simplest men and women as to those best informed about the latest development in philosophical thought.

How and why it fell to women to create this inner renaissance of which the Church as well as the world had the greatest need is what the last of them, Edith Stein, Blessed Teresa Benedicta of the Cross, can best help us understand through her writing on what she called *The Ethos of Women's Vocations*.[1] So let us begin by giving a summary of this important study: undoubtedly she does not say everything to us, but she assuredly gives us a good portion of what is essential.

---

[1] See the analysis of the text summarized here in Oesterreicher, 326ff.

According to Edith, the point of departure is that women do not have that typically masculine narrowness of the specialist. A man will be easily sunk in his business, even more in a cause, expecting from others their interest, their service, but little able to see others and their problems as they are.

An instinctive universality, on the other hand, belongs to the woman.

For the woman, who is not ordinarily as much a prisoner of passing events as men, this adjustment is natural. She can be sympathetically interested in areas where nothing interests her but the fact that they interest those she loves.

Because the man serves his cause more directly, and the woman rather, for him, it is good that she does it under his direction. The obedience that Scripture asks of her is not a whim foreign to the nature of things. In the tree of life, the man represents the trunk, but it is the woman who is at the roots.

Mary, in this respect, is the perfect realization of the woman, as mother and as spouse: her feminine surrender of herself is magnified in Mary's response to the Angel, which is both humble and regal: "Let it be done to me according to your word."

But these feminine talents, perfect in Mary yet, in other women, linked to our fallen nature, are consequently susceptible of being distorted.

The gift of the woman, thus, insofar as it is personal, can become a preoccupation with herself and a desire to share it with others. It can also be turned into an indiscreet, excessive interest in others, into a possessiveness that is no longer truly maternal concern. The sympathetic companion then becomes intrusive, domineering, petty, instead of serving with joy.

Edith advises, as a remedy for this possibility of deterioration, intellectual work and its rigor, provided that the woman does not let herself be shut into a specialization that would be her ruin. But nothing, here, can substitute for divine grace. The woman would benefit particularly from the liturgical life, in which the "we" is substituted for a too-exclusive I. And, above all, the grace that the sacrament brings would free her from all that is restricted to, turned in on, self.

Home life is the proper province of the woman. But there are many excursions outside the family where she will be capable of responding to her feminine vocation: medicine, teaching, social work and all the sciences that have to do with the living, the personal, or that demand a sympathetic penetration into the mind of others.

Indeed, in a field little adapted to her nature, such as a factory, an office, a laboratory, a woman would be able to keep men, who are at an advantage there, from losing their full humanity.

The religious vocation, however, takes on a very particular meaning for the woman. To abandon oneself in love, to become the possession of another and to possess him perfectly in return, is this not the deepest desire of the woman?

If, however, the woman abandons herself in this way to another human being, her abandonment risks perverting her: she becomes the slave of the man, while begging him for what no man can give.

That does not mean that every woman should become a religious, although, when it is her vocation, she finds in it a fulfillment that surpasses all others. But it remains true that it is particularly essential for the woman to become "the servant of the Lord". Whether it is as mother of a family, creator of a household, member of a public profession or cloistered religious, it is always at this that she must succeed in order to be truly fulfilled.

The man, too, of course, is called to serve. But the woman alone can bring to it an essential touch of communion, of reciprocity in personal relations, without which the person is enclosed and strangled in individualism, while society becomes a yoke in which the whole world suffocates. . . .

These few notes apply wonderfully well to all that we have just examined.

In the Middle Ages, when faith tended to be immobilized into a system, when it was not simply a cloak for men who were claiming to serve it while serving only themselves, we have seen Hadewijch remind, laity as well as priests and religious, that the Christian Faith is faith in the living God who gives life but who gives us life only if we open ourselves to the communication of his own life.

Some men after that, like Eckhart and his successors, were able to explain, justify, rationalize her testimony, but not without a great risk of either dissolving it in abstractions or of fitting it into a system of logic in a totally unrealistic way.

It took a thinker who was himself very wise, but basically humble with regard to all paper logic, like Ruusbroec to bring out finally, in all its complementary implications, all of which Hadewijch had had an overall intuition. Other masculine minds, however, more subtle or more distracted by pure logic, had somewhat confused her intuitions while claiming to develop them.

This and more was true for Teresa of Avila. It was Teresa's extraordinary vitality (men never have it to this degree!)

that was necessary to turn upside down a whole institutional Christianity that was exhausted at this point, seemingly incapable of reforming itself without destabilizing itself and either dissolving or becoming hardened. But her exuberant motherliness was not perhaps without some serious risk of confusing a renewed childlikeness and childishness, as we have seen in her indulgence for the charming and inept Gracian. It would take the lucidity, which was colder in appearance, of John of the Cross, her "little Seneca", as she said, to bring out everything but also to preserve everything from threatening confusions in the heritage of the mother of Carmel.

It is very typical, I would say, of the sureness with which women judge each other that daughters of Saint Teresa as unquestionable as Thérèse (the "little" Thérèse in reality is not all that little!) and Elizabeth, who, for her part, seemed like nothing but was all the sharper, were instinctively able to discern that, in the final account, it was John of the Cross they should trust in accepting the whole Cross, without ever losing sight of that *other* world that the Resurrection will allow us to reach.

But, above all, the fearless innocence of Thérèse of Lisieux was necessary to dare return to the essential: the gospel of the divine paternity, which alone can provide the whole meaning, and especially the true meaning, of the Cross.

And the sweet, tranquil obstinacy of Elizabeth, that musician in the soul, was necessary to restore to this discovery itself the unfading joy of praise and the unlimited fullness of this immersion of humanity in the Trinity, which Hadewijch had perceived well but which the mass of doctors who had thrown themselves onto her intuitions had nearly managed (masculine paradox if there ever was one!) to freeze in their intemperate speculations. Finally it was necessary for a woman like Edith, profiting, as she herself advises other women to do, from all that a rigorous intellectual ascesis can bring in the way of clarity, intellectual and moral strength, to restore this rediscovery of the gospel of the Father and the Pauline mystery in universal praise. It is in this, as Pseudo-Dionysius says, that the divine thearchy is extended to the hierarchies of a world invaded, carried along and transported by the Love that is God's alone, who is God alone.

Only the men of the Church, monks like those at Beuron and their Abbot, had been able to provide Edith with the order that this universe presupposes in order to remain authentic, in other words, the apostolic, liturgical structure of the Church. Still, she would perhaps not have grasped it so easily if she had not first submitted to a discipline of thought as austere, as strictly masculine as that of Husserl's phenomenology. And, it goes without saying, with that mixed gift of an ultra-masculine mind, incapable of stopping itself in the development of an overwrought logic, she had been able to cut to the ground the shoots that were only "gourmands" to save the vital growth.

But, in the final analysis, she would not have been capable of any of all that if she had not achieved in her own person, accomplished in the people of God of the First Covenant, the fundamental return to the sources to which the Church of the New must ceaselessly consent if she is not to starve and cease to be herself

And yet, what is lacking in this great woman of intelligence and heart, of whom martyrdom made, as it were, the queen of this line of saints, is a smile.

With Elizabeth, there was to be sure a charming but timid smile: of the artist who forgets herself entirely in her song, to the point of smiling at the Angels while her earthly body is torn and destroyed.

But I will be excused if I say that what convinces me that the second Thérèse is the doctor for whom we have the greatest need is the fact that through all the unbearable tragedy of her ultimate sacrifice, she kept not only a smile but a splendid sense of humor from one end of it to the other. In the worst physical distress, in the suffocating darkness of a faith that was always there but no longer radiated, she never ceased to make fun of herself. Around her, they were already preparing a painted idol, sprinkled with orange-flower water, that they would substitute for her when she had scarcely drawn her last breath. But she spoke in her delectable Norman patois, she did not even shrink from the puns and jokes of the Vermot Almanac! . . . Now that she has finally been delivered from all the papier-maché trifles, in our postconciliar Church, which is bursting with self-criticism and empty self-satisfaction, she is indeed the saint we need!